ST. LOUIS PARKS

ST. LOUIS PARKS

NiNi Harris and Esley Hamilton

Foreword by Peter H. Raven

Photography by Mark Scott Abeln and Steve Tiemann

To Donna,
Happy Birthday,
NiNi
2012

REEDY PRESS
St. Louis, Missouri

Copyright © 2012, Reedy Press
All rights reserved.

Reedy Press
PO Box 5131
St. Louis, MO 63139, USA

Historical photos of St. Louis City parks courtesy Library of Congress,
with the exception of those on pages 2 and 8, which are courtesy the author.
Historical photos of St. Louis County parks courtesy St. Louis County Parks.
Jefferson Barracks aerial photo courtesy Library of Congress.

Library of Congress Control Number: 2012935046

ISBN: 978-1-935806-09-7

Please visit our website at www.reedypress.com.

Design by Nick Hoeing

Printed in the United States of America
12 13 14 15 16   5 4 3 2 1

CONTENTS

ACKNOWLEDGMENTS

S t. Louis Public Library staff members, including Adele Heagney, Cynthia Millar, and Louise Powderly of the History and Genealogy Department, Main Branch, Steve Kozlowski, Library Clerk at Carpenter Branch, and Cynthia E. Jones, Regional Branch Manager, Carpenter Branch, helped locate documents and historical data concerning the development of the Parks and Recreation Department and of individual city parks. Their help was invaluable. Lesley Hoffarth, president and executive director of Forest Park Forever, Carey Bundy of the Great Rivers Greenway, and Grace Fernandez, Ben Nowak, and Tom Sieve of Tower Grove Park provided current data concerning the number and variety of trees in specific parks and usage of local parks. Noel Stasiak related the inspiration for new features in South St. Louis Square Park.

Rich Fernandez, Mary Ann Simon, and Lois Waninger of the Carondelet Historical Society helped locate historical accounts of the parks in the Carondelet area of South St. Louis City. Volunteers with Soulard Restoration Group, Tony Range, George Grove, and Richard Eaton provided information about current uses and landscaping in the Soulard neighborhood parks. Gary D. Bess, director of Parks, Recreation and Forestry, and Daniel W. Skillman, commissioner of Parks, provided historical materials. Sue Clancy, executive director of Forest Park Forever, 1993-1998, recounted the evolution of the master plan for Forest Park and the Restoring the Glory campaign. Dan McGuire, alderman of the 28th Ward, 1981-1997, director of Parks, Recreation and Forestry, 1997-2001, shared his dedication to the parks and his knowledge of their history.

The late Keith Zimmer of the periodicals and microforms department of the St. Louis Public Library was a great help in locating pertinent materials.

Relatively few documents have been published about St. Louis County Parks, so this history owes a great deal to the parks staff who over the years have saved and protected primary documents, in particular Gretta Kraft, Judy Meinershagen, and Susan Poling. To Ben Knox and the many park rangers who compiled the invaluable rangers manual; to Susan Sheppard, who in 2000 researched all the names used in the system; and to Simon Brobbel, who determined park acreage. The scrapbook compilers at the library of the Missouri History Museum have our gratitude for saving things that we missed.

FOREWORD

*P*arks are superb adornments of our modern cities, a mark of civilization at its best and most social. Initially, parks were formed as people moved into cities from farms and felt the need for open space for recreation and clean air. Wise leaders, like many of those whose actions are chronicled in this fascinating book, set aside areas of the disappearing countryside to insure the continuation of the kind of values that were abundantly available to them before they moved into the city. In the pages that follow, we are reminded constantly of the foresight of those who preceded us here in St. Louis.

As the great American landscape architect Frederick Law Olmsted stated in envisioning and planning New York's legendary Central Park, parks are also important places for people from different backgrounds and cultures to meet in neutral surroundings. In Central Park and other parks around the country, they could come together and get to know one another, building together the basis for our richly diverse, heterogeneous society. While individual streets and even whole neighborhoods could remain isolated, parks helped to bring them together.

Parks have been formed, preserved, and enhanced since the early years of the development of St. Louis as a modern city. As the French "common fields" were developed for housing, far-sighted people, starting in the

1830s, began to set aside open areas for the public use, beginning with what is now known as Lafayette Park. The development of additional parks followed in the city, resulting more than one hundred parks! The remarkable images presented here will certainly increase anyone's desire to visit many parks whose features, revealed in this book, will come as a delight and surprise.

In the county, many of the parks have been developed with a natural or semi-natural character. In the years following the Civil War, Americans became aware of their natural surroundings and of our psychological and real dependency on them. Long-established communities in the county sometimes formed their own urban parks, while larger, often partly natural parks were formed as homes and businesses spread over the open ground between the early settlements.

Styles in parks, as in all things, change. A particularly good example of this changing taste is one of the city's great nineteenth-century parks, Tower Grove Park. For the most part, Tower Grove reflects the ideals of park design from long ago and is well preserved, interesting, and approachable for those who enjoy it today. It is important to preserve the structures, styles, and cultural amenities of our parks in such a way as to maintain a diverse, interesting set of them for our enjoyment.

BENTON PARK, ST. LOUIS, MO.

No. 1028. V. O. Hammon Pub. Co., Chicago

With their natural areas, grasslands, and forests, many of the county parks especially are places where children can observe nature and learn about its delicately balanced systems that support us. In the wonder of flowers, insects, grasses, birds, butterflies, and trees, children can become rooted in the natural world and become generally observant in ways that would otherwise not be possible. The importance of parks for children is intuitively understood by us all but is certainly one of the reasons that we cherish and preserve our parks so much. I grew up in San Francisco, when Golden Gate Park and the Presidio beckoned, and the wildlife and plants there certainly nourished my own embryonic love for the diversity of life that so enriches our world.

It should be noted that among America's urban areas, many of the homes in St. Louis are remarkably spread out. A more compact style of housing would allow for even more open space and not disturb so much of the beautiful countryside that surrounds our city in all directions. Still, our style of living is comfortable, a view from above revealing many areas of St. Louis as thickly forested, with houses nestled among the trees and parks standing out as particular jewels among the houses—a very different setting than afforded by New York or San Francisco, but certainly the one that we have inherited. One hopes that in the future even more thought could be given to the construction of comfortable neighborhoods here, set up in such a way as to avoid long-distance commutes as a matter of necessity. In any case, St. Louis will remain a pleasant place to live provided that its citizens care enough to keep it that way. Would not a merger of park systems between the city and the county be a simple and logical way both to effect savings through efficiencies, and to bring together the people of our area even more closely?

Our parks speak to us of the devotion of our ancestors to the public good and the care that they took in making our urban spaces enjoyable for everyone. The parks they established should be preserved for the future, used and enjoyed, and always supported for the general welfare. In this fine book, one can readily see why this is so: The elegant and evocative writing of NiNi Harris and Esley Hamilton brings the history of our rich legacy of parks home to us in an understandable and fascinating way, and the fine images contributed by Mark Scott Abeln and Steve Tiemann will inspire many to undertake their own explorations and enjoy for themselves these remarkable treasures that we hold in trust.

—Peter H. Raven
President Emeritus, Missouri Botanical Garden

CITY PARKS

NiNi Harris

Photography by Mark Scott Abeln

INTRODUCTION

The distinctive fountain that once graced Hyde Park

The definition of St. Louis city parks includes picturesque squares with lush greenery, towering sycamores framing ball fields, and expansive, rolling landscapes with cascading fountains and shimmering lakes. The city boasts more than 100 parks that cover 3,250 acres and are as varied as its neighborhoods. The number and scale of the parks result from the commitment of generations of St. Louisans. This commitment to common spaces dates from when St. Louis was a French village to the ongoing restoration of Forest Park.

Public parks were the stepchild of the Industrial Revolution. Factories meant concentrated jobs, which meant more people, which meant much larger cities. The need for public gardens, yards, and spaces grew with the size of cities—in Europe and America. Young St. Louis, the gateway to a rugged frontier, was a leader in creating parks.

This remarkable park system begins with St. Louis's origins as a French fur trading post in the wilderness. Our French founders organized common fields—land jointly owned and fenced by the villagers. Within the common fields, villagers were assigned strips to cultivate. The result was the system of community ownership and improvement for the common good, a concept similar to nineteenth- and twentieth-century parks.

In 1836, Mayor John Darby scouted wilds far beyond the city limits for a parade ground and park, later named Lafayette Park. The acreage of Lafayette Park, like a number of early parks, was set aside from the common fields for public use. These common-field parks are often said to date to 1812, the year the United States government recognized St. Louis's ownership of the old village's common fields.

Some early parks were donated—Jackson Place in 1816, Carr Square in 1844, and St. Louis Place in 1850. The city purchased the land for Hyde Park in 1854 and transformed an old cemetery to create Benton Park in 1866. By the end of the Civil War, the city owned 287 acres of parks, places, and squares. Then one citizen with a vision for public parks doubled the size of the system. English-born St. Louisan Henry Shaw donated Tower Grove Park and then guided its elegant development.

Citizens and civic leaders debated the advantages of large parks versus small neighborhood parks or squares. Ultimately, St. Louisans established both.

Coinciding with the separation of the city from the county in 1876, the city established three expansive parks on its periphery—179-acre Carondelet Park in far South City, now 127-acre O'Fallon Park in far North City, and one of the largest urban parks in the nation, now 1,293-acre Forest Park.

Unlike the earlier pedestrian parks, Tower Grove, Carondelet, O'Fallon, and Forest parks were the destination of carriage drives. These parks on the outskirts of the city were at first criticized as available only for the well-to-do, distant from working-class neighborhoods. The wisdom of establishing these parks gradually became apparent as they spurred well-planned, handsome residential developments and as mass transit made them accessible to the entire community.

Forest Park in the 1930s—a lily pond with the Chase Park Plaza in the background. When coal smoke clogged the air in the industrialized neighborhoods, park staff and the Red Cross maintained a camp with a community kitchen in Forest Park. St. Louisans from crowded tenements could stay a week at the camp, their summer days spent breathing the fresh air under the shade of mighty trees in Forest Park.

The City Water Division also established two parks in the late nineteenth century. These parks—Reservoir and Chain of Rocks—were created to provide a purified setting, with trees filtering the air around the then-open reservoirs.

Large or small, the city's parks were sylvan retreats that often boasted lush gardens and lakes. These were places for pleasant strolls, carriage rides, picnics, boating, and delightful resorts to join thousands of their neighbors for the popular summer band concerts.

St. Louisans expanded their definition of public parks during the first decade of the twentieth century. Civic leaders recognized that parks could increase the health and happiness of the entire citizenship and physically tie together the disparate city neighborhoods with efficiency and beauty. They developed two major plans that would guide the system's growth for decades—the small park and playground program and the boulevard system.

Small parks were designed to address the shortage of park acreage near downtown and along the river, where most St. Louisans lived. The Civic Plan published in 1907 documented the comparative shortage of park space in this crowded eastern part of the city. While there was one acre of park area to every 97 persons living between Grand Boulevard and the city limits—and there was one acre of park area to every 701 persons living between Grand and Jefferson—between Jefferson Avenue and the river, there was only one acre of park area to every 1,871 persons.

Beginning in 1903, the city began creating pocket parks and playgrounds in the crowded neighborhoods near downtown, along the river, and in its industrial corridor. The city adopted the program of organized play that two local groups—the Wednesday Club and Civic Improvement League—had tested. A new commission for playgrounds and recreation hired

social reformer Charlotte Rumbold as secretary or superintendent of the program. The immediate popularity of the playground program evidenced its importance. Playground attendance during summer school vacation of 1908 averaged 6,798 each day. Attendance at the playgrounds for the year ending in April of 1909 totaled 471,941. The daily cost per child was 1.9 cents. Rolla Wells, who served as mayor from 1901 to 1909, stated that the playground program "was admired and emulated by other cities, and, I think, became the standard of organized public play for the whole nation."

As a consultant to the St. Louis parks, the great landscape architect George Kessler proposed a boulevard system designed to create an emerald necklace of parks and boulevards. In 1907, he proposed ringing St. Louis and connecting its neighborhoods with parks and greenery.

German-born Kessler had emigrated to the United States as a child. He returned to Germany to study landscape gardening and civil engineering.

"The parks are not only for the birds and worms, but primarily for men, women and children, and not only for optical delight, but especially for use for health, happiness and the fostering of a lively public spirit."
—Mayor Rolla Wells

The 1904 World's Fair was constructed over the western half of Forest Park.

Kessler began his career in Kansas City and is credited with that city's park and boulevard system.

The challenge facing Kessler was that the city lies in the shape of an ellipse between the Mississippi and the city limits. The early roads reached out from downtown like spokes on a wheel. Kessler proposed the Kingshighway Boulevard Plan, which followed and extended Kingshighway. The plan connected existing parks, added new parks, and crossed and connected all the spokes or major roads.

Kingshighway was improved and straightened and viaducts were built over rail beds. With its extensions, Kingshighway Boulevard linked Carondelet Park, Tower Grove Park, Forest Park, and the nineteenth-century cemeteries adjacent to O'Fallon Park (Bellefontaine and Calvary)

on the North Side. Bellerive, Christy, and Penrose parks were added along the boulevard system. Parkways in the center of North Kingshighway, and the southeastern extensions of Kingshighway, later renamed Bellerive and Holly Hills boulevards, enhanced the system.

At the same time, Kessler guided the reconstruction of Forest Park after the 1904 World's Fair. Cass Gilbert, architect of the Supreme Court Building and St. Louis's Public Library in downtown, designed the reconstruction of Forest Park's grand basin.

St. Louisan Dwight F. Davis, national tennis doubles champion from 1899 to 1901 and namesake of the Davis Cup in tennis, became commissioner of St. Louis Parks in 1911. Politically a Progressive, this wealthy St. Louisan believed in organized recreation to promote health,

happiness, and build character in all St. Louisans. Davis added tennis courts, golf courses, swimming pools, and ball fields to pastoral retreats with the notion that the city's parks should be utilized to their fullest extent rather than being merely admired.

The resulting system—with expansive parks and small neighborhood parks, formal gardens and natural landscapes, abundant trees that filtered and sweetened the air, sunshowered meadows or fields, plentiful athletic fields for endless hours of fun—served the entire citizenship throughout the twentieth century. That century put extra demands on the park system, and a new commitment to public parks was necessary. A monumental bond

issue in 1923 funded a ribbon of parkway downtown, new neighborhood parks, and improvements to existing parks.

The hardships of the Depression and World War II increased the use of park facilities while resources and manpower were most limited. From 1931 to 1934, the number of large picnics requiring permits increased from 285 to 500. In the summer of 1934, attendance in organized playground programs surpassed one million children. The federally sponsored works programs designed to combat unemployment helped the city address its own shrinking budget to maintain parks during the Great Depression. It also added a new dimension to the parks' landscapes—WPA stonework. Laborers with the Works Progress Administration crafted their distinctive

stonework in parks across the city. They built stone walks and steps that looked as if they were from a land of enchantment. They built white limestone barbeque pits that instantly became landmark features. In small playgrounds, they crafted stone retaining walls that were much more than decorative. The stone walls stopped erosion and added square footage to the valuable play areas.

During World War II, the United States Army built a seventeen-acre recreation camp in the southeastern corner of Forest Park. The camp could accommodate fifteen hundred soldiers. The families of young men fighting the battles of World War II found healthful recreation, distraction, and peace in the city parks.

St. Louisans demonstrated both vision and optimism in 1944—while war still raged in Europe and in the Pacific; while meat, tires, gasoline, and other staples were rationed; and while many of their sons, brothers, and husbands were in harm's way. In this trying and frightening environment, they passed a bond issue to ensure that the parks could be equipped for future generations.

Top: Fairground Park swimming pool.

Bottom: The House of Refuge stood on the site of current-day Marquette Park.

Fairground Park hosted a number of epic soccer matches. Shown here is the 1952-53 CYC final.

to create a new network of trails uniting and enhancing its parks.

While citizens supported their parks, the common spaces were acting as keystones in the rebirth of historic neighborhoods. Lafayette and Benton parks added to the Victorian charm of their historic neighborhoods. In other neighborhoods,

Following the war, baby boomers packed the parks. The postwar building boom filled in the empty lots and edges of the city with more houses and more families. Willmore, Tilles, and Lindenwood parks were developed and dedicated to serve families in these booming neighborhoods of Southwest City. The city acquired the 13.2-acre site of Barrett Brothers Park in the Arlington neighborhood. In 1962, the city developed the Dwight F. Davis Park in the Walnut Park neighborhood.

In recent decades, while the city's population shrank, and while St. Louis faced the challenges that all major American cities have faced, the citizens have repeatedly expressed their love for their parks. In 1993, city voters passed a one-half cent sales tax partly to fund and upgrade their parks. In 2000, they passed proposition C, which created the Metropolitan Parks and Recreation District now known as the Great Rivers Greenway. This new dedicated funding enabled the city to work with surrounding counties to preserve natural lands, restore and improve existing parks, and

proximity to Clifton Heights, Carondelet, and Francis parks kept property values high. Beginning in the 1990s, the parks' new state-of-the-art playgrounds attracted young families.

Citizens helped develop master plans for Carondelet, Forest, Francis, Hyde, and Lafayette parks. The creation of Citygarden in the heart of downtown and the spectacular, ongoing restorations of Tower Grove and Forest parks reflect the same commitment to the common good that guided the development of the remarkable city park system during the nineteenth and twentieth centuries.

While the comprehensive St. Louis city park system serves all neighborhoods in the city, it also can claim two of the nation's outstanding parks. Thanks to massive private donations supplementing tax support, Tower Grove Park ranks as the finest Victorian Park in the nation and Forest Park is praised as the nation's stellar urban park.

LAFAYETTE PARK

*F*ramed by an ornate iron fence topped with fleur-de-lis finials, lush Lafayette Park is one of the oldest parks west of the Mississippi. Created during the Victorian era, the park boasts an enchanting nineteenth-century landscape that is the focal point of its Victorian Lafayette Square neighborhood.

In 1836, St. Louis Mayor John F. Darby reserved the thirty-acre square from the sale of the St. Louis common fields for the park. He described the site as it originally appeared. It was ". . . covered with underbrush of young hickory and oak bushes, and in some places with patches of hazel and sumac bushes. The view of the city, in the distance, from these beautiful grounds was at the time charming indeed."

A city ordinance officially established the park and named it Lafayette Square in 1851. Citizens moving to its vicinity contributed to its improvements. At the beginning of the Civil War, however, the park was used as a military camp. "Beautiful Lafayette Park, with its brilliant flower beds and stretches of green sward, looking like emerald velvet, was turned into a great military camp," St. Louisan Sarah Hill recalled the park in 1861. "Regiments from adjacent states were sent here for organization and drill . . . now campfires were burning. . . . Tents were erected and laid out in streets. It was hot, dry and dusty, and clouds of dust blew and added to the general discomfort."

City financing of park improvements began in 1864. European-trained landscape architect Maximillian G. Kern guided the development of the park. He designed a fantasy land of curious plants, creepers, mosses, beautiful foliage, grottoes, shady nooks, and glades. In 1888, *Commercial and Architectural St. Louis* claimed that

In 1868, the park was embellished by a statue of Senator Thomas Hart Benton by sculptress Harriet Hosmer. Its unveiling was witnessed by a crowd of 40,000 persons. A year later, a bronze copy of Houdon's statue of George Washington was dedicated in the park.

Lafayette Park
Founded: 1836
Size: 30 acres
Cost: Reserved from common fields

Lafayette Park was "one of the handsomest pieces of landscape architecture to be found in the United States."

The most deadly tornado in St. Louis history swept through this idyllic landscape on May 27, 1896. It ripped the mighty shade trees from their roots. It was decades before giant tulip trees, willows, black pines, and elms again shaded the park. In 1927, the *St. Louis Star* described the restored park: ". . . there are quaint by-paths and curious rock work, and shimmering pools in leafy dells waiting to be explored."

The *Star* editorialized against a new threat to the park: "Don't Despoil Lafayette Park," decrying the proposal to use it as an "air landing field" to serve nearby downtown. Then World

War II posed threats with proposals to scrap the park's fence for the metal drive to build tanks. Following the war, and mirroring the neighborhood, the park suffered from deferred maintenance.

Beginning in 1968, as more and more new residents started renovating the nineteenth-century townhouses and mansions surrounding the park, they also began restoring the park's whimsy and charm. Step by step, they restored the damaged finials on the fence, planted an iris garden, and restored the Second Empire–style police station. The park became home to the Vintage Baseball Association. Residents worked with city officials to develop a master plan to guide further enhancements to Lafayette Park.

BENTON PARK

A Victorian pleasure ground, Benton Park spurred the nineteenth-century development of its neighborhood and spurred the restoration of its then historic neighborhood at the turn of the millennium. The park began as the City Cemetery on the road leading to the federal arsenal. When the cemetery was established in 1833, it was far beyond the city's boundaries. Due to the growth and expansion of St. Louis, the graves were moved with reburial at the quarantine section of Arsenal Island in 1856. The year following the Civil War, the city dedicated the old cemetery as a park in the new, developing South City area. The park was named for Missouri's first senator and proponent of Manifest Destiny, Thomas Hart Benton.

As park keeper, German immigrant and horticulturist Edward Krausnick transformed the abandoned cemetery into a luxuriant 14.3-acre park. The city financed his efforts, spending almost $93,000 on Benton Park during the Gilded Age. As the red-brick German neighborhood grew up around the park, the park itself became "confessedly one of the most beautiful attractions of the City," according to *Commercial and Architectural St. Louis*.

Reflecting the German character of the new neighborhood in 1882, citizens dedicated a granite obelisk in Benton Park honoring German-American Colonel Friedrich Hecker. This patriot raised a regiment of local German-Americans during the Civil War, serving first under General John C. Fremont and later commanding his own brigade in the Union Army. Germanic St. Louisan, architect Ernest C. Janssen, designed the shaft of the monument.

Benton Park
Founded: 1866
Size: 14.3 acres
Cost: Former City Cemetery

During the 1890s, South St. Louisans flocked to the park for the summer concerts held on Saturday nights. The evolution of the surrounding urban neighborhood and of the cemetery into an urban resort was clear in the description in the annual report of 1900. "The park, although in the midst of a thickly built-up part of the city, is a delightful retreat. The ground is naturally very broken, and with its two lakes, grotto, Hecker monument, music stand, shaded walks, and lily pond, forms a favorite resort on the South Side."

The surrounding blocks are now part of an historic district named for Benton Park that began experiencing a remarkable rejuvenation in the 1990s. New residents restoring nearby houses treasure their views of the romantic park. Though the park activities have changed—the Gateway Classic bike race has replaced the Victorian band concerts—the annual report on Benton Park from the spring of 1914 is as true today as it was then. The park's "beauty and attractiveness is one of the joys of the people living near this section on the south side, and has aroused a most appreciative neighborhood pride."

TOWER GROVE PARK

*T*ower Grove Park—filled with ornamental trees, giant shade trees, curving carriage drives, statuary, Victorian follies, and stone gates at every drive and walkway—seems a mythical land.

One of the finest examples of Victorian landscape in the nation, Tower Grove Park's nearly three hundred acres also shows traces of St. Louis's French heritage. Its long, narrow footprint reflects the long, narrow, east-west strips of the colonial-era common field that it was cut from.

Anglo-American businessman and philanthropist Henry Shaw donated the park to the people of St. Louis in 1868. In concert with St. Louis's premier mid-nineteenth-century architect George I. Barnett, a fellow Anglo-American, Shaw guided its development during the next two decades. He believed that trees were "the grand ornaments of every rural scene, and much more conducive to the pleasure and enjoyment of the public than any artificial structures that can be erected by the hand of man. . . ." So he transformed the almost treeless prairie into a wooded landscape that today boasts 7,653 trees of 222 species.

Between 1871 and 1873, Shaw and his team dotted the landscape with a dozen gazebos, or shelters. There are octagonal gazebos, gazebos topped with lacy ornamental ironwork, gazebos topped by cupolas, gazebos with Gothic arches. One features an onion-domed roof, and another is fashioned after a Chinese pagoda.

Each of the park's ten gateways is unique. Sculptures of griffins and sleeping lions top the stone piers of the east carriage gate. The castle-like west carriage gate has forty-foot-tall crenellated stone towers. This Gothic-style gate reflects the

Tower Grove Park
Founded: 1868
Size: 289 acres
Cost: Gift of Henry Shaw

Victorian fascination with the chivalrous tales of knights. Shaw salvaged the smooth stone columns of the north gate from the Old Courthouse when it was being remodeled in 1870.

The most whimsical folly of the park is the mock ancient ruins that form the backdrop for the fountain pond. The ruins were built with architectural salvage from the burned Lindell Hotel in 1867. Statuary honoring musicians, writers, and scientists are focal points within the park.

The flower beds around statuary and gates are planted with ornamental grasses, canna lilies, castor beans, flowering tobacco, and other plantings popular during the Victorian era. A series of amoeba-shaped lily ponds are filled with fragrant water lilies that bloom each September.

The park's trees, flower beds, and historic buildings were restored and are now maintained in Victorian style with a combination of city funds and the generosity of the supporters and Friends of Tower Grove Park.

In 1989, Tower Grove Park attained the status

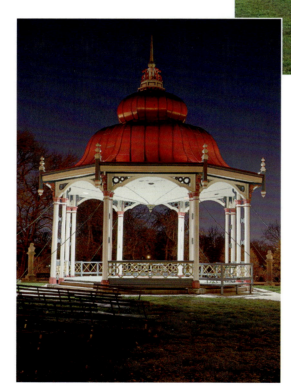

only enjoyed by four other parks in the nation. It was declared a National Historic Landmark.

The museum-like quality of the park attracts visitors from around the nation while holding an almost magical appeal for St. Louisans. On summer Saturdays there are rows of limousines as brides line up for wedding pictures posed in the park's "ruins." Thousands picnic around the Victorian bandstand during the Musical Monday concerts. Even kickball players lobby for the privilege to use the park's sporting fields.

Henry Thiele, Francis Tunica, and Eugene Greenleaf formed a team of architects who assisted Henry Shaw and George I Barnett in developing the park.

FOREST PARK

*F*ifty thousand people gathered on June 24, 1876, to dedicate Forest Park. Many thought paying $849,058 for a nearly fourteen hundred-acre swath of land on the unpopulated outskirts of St. Louis was wasteful foolishness. Forest Park, however, would enrich life for generations of St. Louisans, it would become home to our cultural institutions and evolve into one of the nation's great urban jewels. After a massive hundred million-dollar park restoration that began in the mid-1990s, Forest Park reigns as the nation's stellar urban park.

St. Louisans began promoting the idea of an expansive park while Confederate armies still threatened the city. There were debates and legal actions, but park promoters would not be deterred.

They chose an immense tract of rolling terrain, its contours broken by hills and covered by virgin forest. Only a few neglected farms and abandoned huts of coal miners defaced the vast expanse of natural forest.

The landscape architect of Lafayette Park, Maximillian Kern, designed improvements for Forest Park. The result was a driving park with winding roads, rustic bridges, and lakes. Bandstands, pagodas, and picnic grounds interspersed the sylvan setting.

The park was chosen as part of the site of the Louisiana Purchase Exposition, and construction began in 1901. For the Fair, the park's western half was transformed into a veritable fairyland of white palaces surrounded by lagoons and artistic landscaping that extended west to Big Bend Boulevard. The magnificent spectacle attracted 20 million visitors.

Forest Park
Founded: 1876
Size: 1,293 acres, originally 1,380
Cost: $849,058

After the Fair, the famous landscape architect George Kessler guided the artful reconstruction of the park that included four great memorials from the Fair—the World's Fair Pavilion completed at a cost of $40,000 in 1909; the Fair's Fine Arts Palace designed by Cass Gilbert became the Saint Louis Art Museum; an equestrian statue of St. Louis known as the "Apotheosis of St. Louis" was presented in 1906; and, in 1913, the Jefferson Memorial. The massive birdcage was preserved from the Fair. One by one, cultural institutions moved to or opened in the park.

When Dwight F. Davis became park commissioner in 1911, he focused on athletics and recreational facilities. In Forest Park, he added thirty-two tennis courts in 1912. Spreading lawns were transformed into soccer and baseball fields. He guided construction of an additional golf course. While golf was known as a rich man's game, a Forest Park tournament attracted players from the most exclusive country clubs as well as from the professions, stock rooms, and machine shops. In 1918, the cost of maintaining the golf courses came to just over six cents per game.

Davis established a tradition of recreational use. By 1929, the park was home to thirty-eight tennis courts, two public golf courses, twenty baseball diamonds, two soccer fields, two handball courts, a croquet course, a cricket lawn, and an archery range.

Massive tree-planting restored the forest canopy to the former fairgrounds. By the spring of 1934, Forest Park's trees numbered 45,450, in varieties "too numerous to mention," according to city forester Ludwig Baumann.

Following the Second World War, the cultural institutions located in Forest Park thrived: the Saint Louis Art Museum located in the Fair's Fine Arts Palace; McDonnell Planetarium, dedicated in 1963, was transferred to the St. Louis Science Center in the 1980s; the Missouri Historical Society located in the Jefferson Memorial; the Muny Opera opened with *Aida* in 1917; the Saint Louis Zoo organized in 1911.

Forest Park, however, suffered slow decline. Suburban and sprawl development spread the population and taxpayers over a large metro area, but only the citizens within the limited St. Louis City boundaries supported the park and its institutions. In 1972, voters

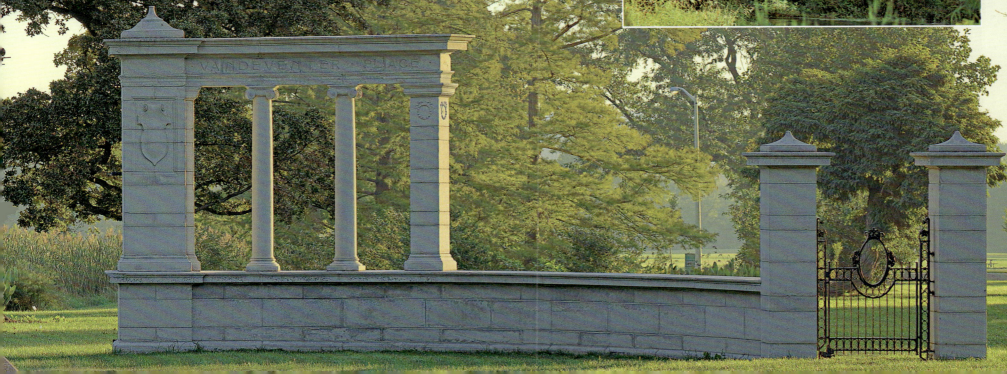

established the Zoo Museum District. As a result, city and county residents supported the Zoo, Art Museum, and later the Science Center and History Museum with their tax dollars.

The park itself, however, was supported only by city residents, a fraction of the population using it. During the 1950s, 250 city employees worked full-time in Forest Park. By the 1970s, only 25 part-time employees maintained the huge park.

In the mid-1980s, the city of St. Louis established Forest Park Forever, a non-profit organization dedicated to restoring, maintaining, and sustaining Forest Park. The city and Forest Park Forever worked with thousands of citizens to develop a master plan for the park that was adopted in 1995. The plan adapted the park's facilities to current needs while restoring historical features and enhancing the natural environments.

Fountains and formal balustrades were added to the Grand Basin at the foot of Art Hill. Using the natural terrain, the water features—lakes, streams, waterfalls, and fountains—were expanded while water use was cut in half. Savannahs and prairies were restored, adding habitat for wildlife. The park's trees, currently numbering about 15,000 in manicured areas and about 30,000 in natural areas, provide lush canopies and a rich environment for a growing variety of birdlife.

The result is that Forest Park sparkles, dazzling 12 million visitors each year.

CARONDELET PARK

The waves and swells in the landscape shaded by century-old trees give Carondelet Park, at the city's southeast corner, its distinctive character. The park—destination of thousands of twenty-first-century bicyclers, walkers, and soccer players—was dedicated on July 4, 1876, as one of the trio of large parks developed in the 1870s.

To assemble the acreage, the city purchased land from speculators. Except for Alexander Lacy Lyle's elegant, white-frame antebellum home at the center of the park, the land was undeveloped.

A picnic pavilion was built, and private donations funded an artificial boat lake in the 1890s. The park's natural features, however, were its attractions. A *Souvenir of Carondelet*, published in the early 1890s, noted the park's "noble growth of oak, walnut and hickory trees. . . ." The land itself was exotic, with sinkholes that had formed over the centuries as the underlying limestone slowly eroded. In 1900, the parks annual report described the grounds as "an ideal place for a park, with its high elevation, undulating surface, natural grottoes, springs and sink holes."

Over the next four decades, the city gradually added features and architectural amenities to the park's natural attractions. The water surface of the boat lake was doubled in 1909. Three years later, a series of eight sinkholes were hooked together to create the quarter-mile-long Horse Shoe Lagoon.

In 1913, the Arts and Crafts–style Grand Boulevard viaduct was constructed at the park's entrance. The city began building the handsome two-story boathouse

overlooking the lake in 1918. The 1920s saw the construction of the Arts and Crafts–influenced, two-story, brick stables with extended eaves supported by wood brackets.

During the Great Depression, WPA workers further improved the park with their distinctive stonework. Their features included stone walls, stone steps leading to the lake, and a charming stone bridge over Horse Shoe Lagoon.

The park became a favorite setting for school picnics during the mid-twentieth century. For generations, Carondelet Park has hosted family reunions and has been the place where senior citizens teach their grandchildren to fish. Since the millennium, new walking and bike paths have increased use of the park by people enjoying a Sunday stroll, competitive bikers, and runners. On Sundays, 15 to 150 young people wearing tunics gather in the shade of Carondelet's mighty trees. With imitation, foam-covered swords they reenact medieval warfare.

The city has planted a thousand new trees in thirty-three species—ensuring the lush, green canopy sheltering Carondelet Park for future generations of fishermen and picnickers.

O'FALLON PARK

*A*placid lake, reflecting its sprawling Florentine-style boathouse, graces O'Fallon Park—one of a trio of parks established on the outskirts of St. Louis in 1876.

This North Side park offered "a prominent position on the bluffs, and a commanding view of the extensive valley and waters of the Mississippi," according to L. U. Reavis's 1875 book *Saint Louis*. Since the construction of I-70 in 1954, the park is recognized as the well-treed hills rising on the west side of the interstate.

The parkland was part of the estate of the late Colonel John O'Fallon. A veteran of the War of 1812, O'Fallon became an assistant Indian agent in St. Louis. He prospered as a sutler, or contractor supplying the frontier army. O'Fallon invested wisely in early railroads, the gas company, and in real estate. He built his own brick country home atop the hills that are now parkland and named it Athlone in honor of his father's hometown in Ireland. Excavation for the home uncovered bones, arrowheads, stone axes, and utensils, indicating it was an Indian mound.

The city purchased 158 acres from O'Fallon's children. The site is complemented by adjacent Bellefontaine and Calvary cemeteries. The Rural Cemetery Movement, which introduced landscape design to cemeteries, inspired the development of both these institutions. Their monuments melted into the landscapes as the roads followed the natural contours of the land.

O'Fallon Park became a destination for carriage rides, as evidenced by the installation of fountains to water horses in 1893. The lake, constructed two years later, covers 6.5 acres. It featured a landscaped island. Later, a stone wall was built

O'Fallon Park
Founded: 1876
Size: 127 acres, originally 158
Cost: $259,065

around the island to stop erosion, and it became one of the lake's decorative features.

Glens, picturesque ravines, a turn-of-the-century observatory, tennis courts, and ball fields turned the park into a mecca for pleasure seekers. Permits document the early twentieth-century popularity of the park—289 picnic permits and over 2,000 permits for the tennis courts issued during the summer of 1911 alone. During 1912, O'Fallon Park was the scene of 45,525 tennis games.

The boathouse dates to 1913, and the two-story brick stable was constructed in 1925. The park's thick canopy included 4,463 trees, according to a 1934 survey.

While the donation of an abandoned adjacent cemetery added 8.5 acres to the park, the state took acreage for the construction of Interstate 70.

Civic leaders see a new role for this historic park— as a catalyst for strengthening and restoring its surrounding historic neighborhood. As part of this vision, in 2011, three hundred new trees were planted to ensure the park's forest canopy. New trails were constructed through the rolling acres of greenery. Immediately, park use increased as walkers and hikers rediscovered the beauties of O'Fallon Park, its picturesque boathouse, and ancient trees.

FRANCIS PARK

Francis Park is the keystone of the St. Louis Hills neighborhood. It is also where nature, recreation, art, music, and neighbors meet.

Created in the twentieth century in a setting influenced by the Art Deco Movement, this remarkable park bears a strong resemblance to Victorian-era Lafayette Park. Like its Victorian counterpart, Francis Park is square and designed for walking, not driving. It is surrounded by broad boulevards lined with impressive architecture.

Real estate developer Cyrus Crane Willmore used the park as a selling point for his lots and houses in the St. Louis Hills neighborhood. He reserved lots facing the park's corners for churches, which accent the park's design.

The parkland was mostly in a natural state in 1930 when Park Commissioner Fred Pape predicted that Francis was "destined to be one of the beauty spots of St. Louis." Sixty thousand dollars was dedicated to developing the park, including massive grading and tree planting. By the spring of 1934, the city forester reported that the trees in Francis Park numbered 2,458. With manpower supplied by the Civil Works Administration (CWA) and the Works Projects Association (WPA) relief programs, the park commissioner could report in the spring of 1937 that Francis Park was 85 percent complete. Over ninety thousand square feet of sidewalks and athletic facilities, including handball, horseshoe, and tennis courts, were constructed. The relief workers constructed a four hundred-foot-long rectangular lily pond that was filled with water lilies and their rosy bursts of color.

Francis Park
Founded: 1917
Size: 60 acres
Cost: Gift of David R. Francis

The park itself features old groves of Austrian pines, Scotch pines, and Norway spruce. There are abundant sycamores and giant pin oaks, which are the landscape signature of the neighborhood. Allées of bald cypress line the central walks framing the lily pond. The northeast corner of the park features a landscape with characteristic WPA stonework. A curving stone bench was built into a sloping hillside, and small, rustic stone bridges cross the rivulet streaming through that corner of the park.

In 1884, civic leader David R. Francis purchased farmland, including the park site, that had originally been part of a Spanish land grant. Francis is best remembered for his dynamic leadership as president of the 1904 Louisiana Purchase Exposition. His resume, however, included mayor of the city of St. Louis, governor of the state of Missouri, and secretary of the interior in the Cabinet of President Grover Cleveland. While Francis was serving as ambassador to Tsarist Russia, he officially donated the parkland to the city.

In addition to the steady use of the handball and tennis courts, in recent decades the park has developed a regional following that daily fills the park with recreational walkers. Beginning in 2002, residents commissioned a series of sculptures for the park. Eleven sparkling mosaic-covered works inspired by fairy tales ornament the lily pond area. Residents sponsored their first Art in the Park fair in 2005, which is fostering more original art for Francis Park. Attendance at the Sunday Serenades of the Compton Heights Concert Band, begun in Francis Park in 1986, averages three thousand. With its constant hum of activity, this park is the ultimate community common ground.

KINGSHIGHWAY PARKS

At the beginning of the twentieth century, a series of new parks and boulevards were created as part of the Kingshighway Boulevard system. The Kingshighway system looped the city, connecting existing and adding new parks. The system began at Bellerive Park with its spectacular riverviews. The loop concluded at Bellefontaine Cemetery, adjacent to O'Fallon Park with its commanding view of the Mississippi. Kingshighway and its extensions—Holly Hills and Bellerive boulevards—hooked together Forest, Carondelet, and Tower Grove parks. Three more new parks—Bellerive, Christy, and Penrose—were designed as links in this emerald necklace.

The Kingshighway Boulevard system made each park more accessible to the entire region. Sadly, in the 1960s the construction of Interstate 55 severed the boulevard system from its dramatic starting place, Bellerive Park.

BELLERIVE PARK

Bluff-top Bellerive Park offers spectacular vistas of the Mississippi River. The park's main entrance is over a broad stuccoed bridge constructed in 1917. Ten years after the bridge was built, the city constructed the Mission-style pavilion with its trio of arches framing views of the river.

Bellerive Park
Founded: 1908
Size: 5.6 acres
Cost: $110,422

CHRISTY PARK

Wedge-shaped Christy Park was purchased in 1910 as part of the arc of parkland connecting Holly Hills Boulevard with Kingshighway. Christy Park and Boulevard followed a narrow creek bed valley. It evolved as a ribbon of trees, lawns, and fields. The 1934 CWA survey reported that Christy Park already boasted 1,390 trees. In 1999, sixteen acres of the park were renamed Joseph R. Leisure Park. A dedicated public servant, Leisure began his career as a grasscutter and rose to serve as the city parks commissioner. Children of South City's Bosnian community especially enjoy the playground in this park.

THE CHRISTY GREENWAY

This linear park designed for walkers and bikers follows the creek bed valley that connects Christy Park to the River des Peres Parkway. Historic Sts. Peter & Paul Cemetery and Gatewood Gardens Cemetery line part of the greenway. With their white and gray stones and monuments, they create a sculpture garden as a backdrop. The Christy Greenway is the work of the Great Rivers Greenway.

The Christy Greenway
Founded: 2005
Size: 1 mile
Cost: Donated

Christy Park
Founded: 1910
Size: 32 acres
Cost: $95,504

PENROSE PARK

When the city purchased the acreage at North Kingshighway and Bircher as a North City link in the Kingshighway system, the surrounding area was undeveloped. The Parks' Report of 1912 envisioned that Penrose "will ultimately become a neighborhood park and play field, when the surrounding properties are improved with homes." A century later, the surrounding area is an historic neighborhood.

Kingshighway Boulevard and railroad tracks divide this park into quadrants. The Mathews-Dickey Boys Club calls a quadrant home. In 1961, the St. Louis Cycling Club built the one-fifth-mile velodrome, known as the "Penrose Park Bowl," in one of the quadrants. The banked bicycle course was the scene of the 1962 National Cycling Championships. After falling into disrepair, enthusiasts recently raised the money to repave the track.

Penrose Park
Founded: 1910
Size: 51 acres
Cost: $165,127

WILLMORE PARK

The normally peaceful landscape of Willmore Park occasionally transforms into a joyously noisy place when the barking from the patrons of the dog park is added to the cheers from the ball fields and combines with the raucous honking from flocks of geese.

Though it is one of the city's newest major parks, Willmore Park has already made lots of good memories. Neighborhood residents can't help but smile when they talk about Camp Willy Worm or Camp Funny Face, summer camps held in Willmore Park during the 1980s that taught city kids how to sail in catamarans on the park's lakes.

This long, sweeping park borders the St. Louis Hills neighborhood and is the companion park to the River des Peres Parkway. Willmore follows the inside of the River des Peres's broad curve. The River des Peres Parkway follows the outer bank of the stone-sided river channel, and its line of trees provide a backdrop of green vistas for Willmore Park visitors.

Willmore Park originated with Cyrus Crane Willmore, the developer of the St. Louis Hills neighborhood, donating seventy acres on the perimeter of the St. Louis Hills neighborhood for the park. The real estate developer stipulated that the city acquire and dedicate the balance of the 105 acres, making Willmore Park the sixth largest park in the city. The transfer of the deed to the land required that the city start clearing, grading, and landscaping the area on or before June 1, 1947. Willmore also stipulated that the strip of land never be used for an airport.

Willmore Park
Founded: 1947
Size: 105 acres
Cost: 70 acres donated, $52,000
for remaining acreage

Landscape architect Stuart M. Mertz in association with Layton, Layton, and Rodes designed the park, locating the roadways around the perimeter.

The popularity of Willmore Park's playground, fields, bicycle and running trail, and picnic shelters is due to the rolling landscape. Groves of mighty trees shade its large lawns. Shimmering lakes, one covering three acres and the other covering five, seem constantly rippling with the maneuvers of dozens of ducks and geese.

GATEWAY MALL

*A*long, narrow strip of parks and public spaces, planned and developed over a century, form downtown's Gateway Mall. It stretches along Market Street from the grounds of the Gateway Arch to the western edge of downtown past 20th Street. At the eastern end, the sunken garden of Luther Ely Smith Park, maintained by the National Park Service, connects the Arch with the Old Courthouse.

Immediately west of the Courthouse is 1.9-acre Kiener Plaza, created by a city ordinance in 1962. The acquisition cost for the prime location was $2 million. A St. Louis businessman, civic leader, and amateur athlete, Harry Kiener donated a circular fountain as the centerpiece. The statue of "The Runner" is at the center of the twenty-five-foot-wide fountain. Ancient ruins inspired the Morton D. May Amphitheater, built in 1987 at 6th Street. The sunken amphitheater with rolling fountains is a popular stage for wedding photos.

Citygarden covers two blocks, or the three acres of the Mall from 8th to 10th streets. Funded by the Gateway Foundation, this interactive sculpture garden features modern and contemporary sculptures. Their backdrops are provided by fountains and native Missouri trees, shrubs, grasses, groundcovers, and wildflowers. The fountains include a six-foot cascade over native limestone, a splash plaza with 102 vertical jets, and a tilted granite disk that moves water gently from the base of a massive sculpture.

Richard Serra's sculpture, "Twain," dominates the next block of the Mall. Its forty-foot steel panels were installed in 1982.

The Gateway Mall extending west from 12th Street to Union Station, known collectively as Memorial Plaza, consists of parks, fountains, and memorials. Poelker Park, Memorial Plaza Parks, Kaufmann Park, and Eternal Flame Park create this grouping. Memorial Plaza originated with a plan in 1904 for impressive civic buildings connected by a central plaza. The plaza links and offers vistas of St. Louis's grand City Hall, Public Library, and Union Station. The $87 million bond issue of 1923 included development of this park space and the building of Soldier's Memorial at its heart. During the 1930s, dramatic Art Deco–style civic buildings were constructed around the plaza. Memorials honor St. Louis's firefighters, policemen, and St. Louisans who served in the Korean War and in World War II.

Aloe Plaza, the block facing Union Station framed by 18th and 20th streets, was cleared to serve as a stage for the stunning Milles Fountain. Officially named "The Meeting of the Waters," the fountain depicts the confluence of the Missouri and Mississippi rivers. The great Swedish sculptor Carl Milles created the fountain with fourteen bronze figures in a rectangular pool of black and salmon marble measuring two hundred feet by thirty-five feet. When it was unveiled in 1940, the provocative fountain was considered scandalous. The Aloe Plaza Extension covers the block to the west of 20th Street.

FAIRGROUND PARK

The castle-like façade of the old bear pits still guards the southeast corner of Fairground Park. It recalls the park's heritage as the St. Louis Agricultural and Mechanical Fairgrounds. Beginning in 1856, the annual fair drew visitors from across the region. In 1860, 150,000 people crammed the fairgrounds to see the Prince of Wales, the future King Edward VII of England. Eventually, the fairgrounds included an art gallery, racetrack, mechanical hall, and zoological gardens.

Competing with new attractions, the fair's popularity gradually faded. In 1908, the city bought the then-vacant fairgrounds and transformed it into a public park.

On July 15, 1913, the Parks Department opened a swimming pool surrounded by a sand beach in Fairground Park. The pool covered five acres, making it the largest outdoor pool in the world. The operating costs were considered high, ninety-five dollars a day, but justified. More than a half-million men, women, and children used the pool in the first two months.

A 1949 confrontation between neighborhood African-American and white youth over the desegregation of the park's swimming pool was an important test of public access in St. Louis's history. The bond issue that passed in 1955 paid for a new swimming pool, hard-surface tennis courts, and lighted baseball diamonds.

Fairground Park
Founded: 1908
Size: 131 acres
Cost: $700,000

LYON PARK

Office workers from nearby industries and agencies treasure the quiet green acres of Lyon Park for walks and runs and as a lunchtime retreat. Facing South Broadway opposite castle-like Anheuser-Busch Brewery, this park slopes down to the complex of stone and brick buildings that houses a division of the National Geospatial-Intelligence Agency. These acres, however, were not always the peaceful retreat between hubs of activity. For decades, the park acreage bustled and hummed.

Beginning in 1827, these acres were part of a U.S. arsenal supplying the Armies of the West. Hundreds of laborers produced, repaired, and stored arms. They supplied Fremont's expeditions and American troops who battled in the War with Mexico.

The arsenal was a coveted prize at the beginning of the Civil War. Captain Nathaniel Lyon, an ardent abolitionist, commanded the arsenal, organized German volunteers for the Union Army, and protected the munitions. Activity at the arsenal increased as the war became more fierce and more costly. By 1865, a thousand men worked there.

The War Department transferred nearly eleven acres of the arsenal to the city for Lyon Park, memorializing the Union commander. The city planted lawns and shade trees and commissioned and installed the obelisk honoring General Nathaniel Lyon.

During August of 1913, area families brought mattresses and pillows to the park. Because it was in a crowded neighborhood with few yards, the park commission had designated Lyon as the South Side park to be used by sleepers on hot nights.

Lyon Park
Founded: 1868
Size: 10.92 acres
Cost: Gift of federal government

CLIFTON HEIGHTS PARK

The origin of this saucer-shaped park set at the foot of rippled slopes mirrors that of nineteenth-century Methodist campgrounds.

In 1885, a group of Methodists and their pastor, the Reverend Benjamin St. James Fry, bought thirty-five acres in what was then an isolated area of Southwest St. Louis. They commissioned St. Louis's premier designer of private places, Julius Pitzman, to survey and plat the area. He designed streets that curve irregularly to match the hilly terrain. In the style of the campgrounds, he left a large green, or commons, at the base of the valley. During the following decades, rambling frame houses were built on the slopes overlooking the idyllic commons.

The camp's commons was conveyed to the city in 1912 for a park. The Parks Department constructed a small lake. The annual report of 1913 described the inviting lake as "adding to the beauty of this little place." In the early 1920s, the city bought adjoining property, enlarging the park to its present size, 4.4 acres.

The department described the progress made in Clifton Heights Park in their annual report of 1928. "At last its beauty is completed. Nestling cozily in its luxurious growth and quaint surroundings it truly is one of the beauty spots in St. Louis. . . ."

The water system for the picturesque lake, however, created some unpleasantness in the neighborhood. This was corrected in 1944, when the Parks Department "overhauled water mains & valves, thereby eliminating objectionable noises in the private plumbing of the neighborhood homes. . . ."

HYDE PARK

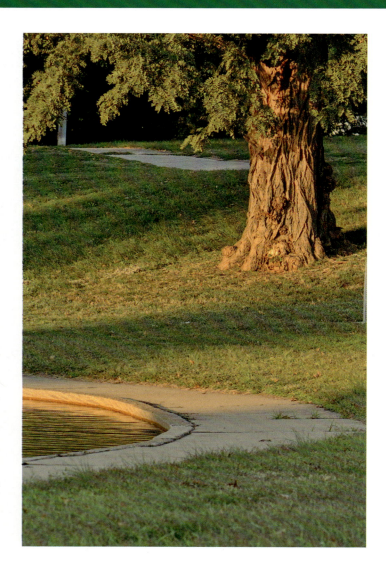

*O*nly the gazebo with the onion-domed roof remains to recall the Victorian landscape that once filled this twelve-acre square. Yet this small park is rich with history.

When the city established Hyde Park, it marked a new dedication to creating a park system. All the earlier parkland had been donated or reserved from the old common fields. This was the first time the city was required to pay for parkland.

The park site had been part of the North Side real estate of Dr. Bernard Farrar, the first American physician to settle in St. Louis after the Louisiana Purchase. In 1850, his widow subdivided the property. The park and subdivision were apparently named for London's Hyde Park.

To pay for park improvements, the city rented the land—for a vegetable garden and then as a beer garden, with the old Farrar mansion serving as a hotel and inn.

During the Civil War, the park was the site of political and patriotic gatherings. On July 4, 1863, while great battles were being waged at Gettysburg and Vicksburg, thousands crowded into Hyde Park. The patriotic celebration devolved into a deadly riot between convalescing Union troops and Confederate sympathizers.

Landscaping of the park began in 1874. It was directed by Theodore Link, later known as the architect of Union Station. By the end of the Victorian era, an elegant fountain, an artificial lake, and a bandstand added to the park's allure.

The tornado of 1927 destroyed much of Hyde Park's Victorian character.

Hyde Park
Founded: 1854
Size: 12 acres
Cost: $36,250

SOULARD POCKET PARKS

The Soulard neighborhood boasts two delightful pocket parks—Soulard Park next to Soulard Market and Pontiac Park at 9th and Ann streets. These parks, favorites with public gardeners and the neighborhood's many dog lovers, share a common origin. They were both proposed in the 1907 Civic Plan with the goal of providing playground areas in the then-overcrowded immigrant community.

A 1906 bond issue paid for the valuable land. The city cleared the commercial buildings, graded the blocks, and was operating playgrounds on them by 1911. The use of these parks was staggering. Between April of 1919 and April of 1920 alone attendance at playground activities numbered 128,024 children in Pontiac Park and another 74,117 children in Soulard Park. In 1938, the city used WPA workers and resources to build the stone terraces and retaining walls around the small parks.

As the neighborhood became revitalized in the late twentieth century, the pocket parks took on new roles. Soulard Park hosts the annual Wiener Derby, or the Daschund race, held after the dog parade, kicking off the Mardi Gras celebration.

Beginning in 1990, volunteers with the Soulard Restoration Group have been gardening in these parks and giving Pontiac Park a unique aesthetic. Volunteers have filled beds and stone-edged terraces with flowering shrubs, ornamental grass, and evergreens. In Victorian fashion, neighborhood associations have framed these pocket parks with decorative iron fencing.

Pontiac Park
Founded: 1908
Size: 1.9 acres
Cost: $94,256

Soulard Park
Founded: 1908
Size: 1.9 acres
Cost: $174,580

DUTCHTOWN PARKS

*T*hree small parks in the Dutchtown neighborhood of South St. Louis—Gravois, Laclede, and Mount Pleasant parks—share a common history and role in their communities. These green and shaded squares serve their middle-class, brick neighborhood as extended community backyards. Like backyards, two of the parks, Laclede and Mount Pleasant, face alleys.

Their origins date to 1812 when their neighborhoods were simply wilderness, miles beyond the fur-trading post of St. Louis. That year, the United States recognized public ownership of the French common fields, land that had been jointly owned by early settlers of St. Louis. While the city of St. Louis was gradually selling the common fields, civic leaders saved these three squares for public or park use.

Gravois Park, near Grand and Gravois, became home to a huge neighborhood Independence Day celebration beginning in 1910. The octagonal bandstand, in then new-style concrete construction with a Mission tile roof, was built in 1924.

Little Laclede Park is near South Broadway and Gasconade Street. Neighbors enjoy its abundance of lawns and shade trees.

Mount Pleasant Park, near Michigan Avenue at Dakota Street, was originally called Dakota Park and became a popular playground for the children of the nearby Polish community. During the summer of 1917, attendance at this little park's playground surpassed 37,000.

Dutchtown Parks
Founded: 1854
Size: Gravois - 8.2 acres
Laclede - 3.17 acres
Mount Pleasant - 3.17 acres
Cost: Set aside from common fields

RIVER DES PERES PARKWAY

*T*his ribbon of green, which doubles as a boulevard, provides ball fields, playgrounds, and an enticing trail. Lush trees shade these features. A parkway following the outer bank of the River des Peres was first proposed a century ago and has evolved over three quarters of a century. Landscape architect George Kessler encouraged creating a parkway in a sweeping arc around the southwest border of the city in 1911. He wrote that the River des Peres Valley, from practically the Mississippi River to McCausland Avenue, offered ". . . an opportunity, . . . to establish a splendid parkway, that would supply a tie along the western border of the city that cannot be surpassed. . . ."

The city purchased the riverside acreage in 1934, and its initial development was completed during the Great Depression. Over 12,000 shrubs and more than 2,500 trees were planted along the linear park. Eight hundred American elm trees lined both sides of the driveway. In 1938, the Parks Department annual report stated, "A new parkway, . . . immediately on the county border, has been completed and developed into a beautiful Parkway. This parkway ranges in width from 250 feet to 1,000 feet." The park and boulevard was extended south of Gravois, with an average width of twenty feet on each side of the driveway.

In 2005, the parkway's new tree-lined bike and hiking trails were completed. Along with stone entrances and gates featuring 44 stone columns, the 5.5-mile trail (including the Christy Greenway) features a 250-foot-long pedestrian bridge crossing the River des Peres. As part of the development of this trail, 1,718 new trees were planted.

The River des Peres Parkway is the city's fifth-largest park. With its new plantings, trails, and distinctive stone gateways, it has become one of the city's newest green meccas, attracting bicyclers from the entire region.

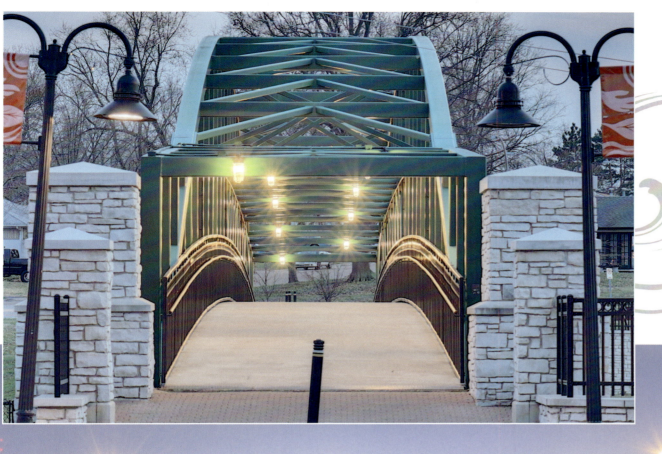

River des Peres Parkway
Founded: 1934
Size: 145 acres
Cost: Donated

MARQUETTE PARK

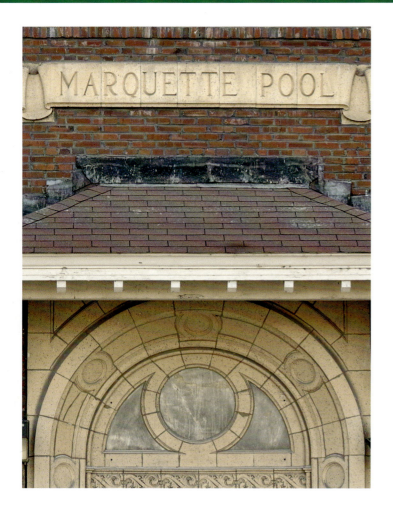

*M*arquette Park, in the heart of the South Side's Dutchtown neighborhood, was the site of a makeshift hospital for Civil War soldiers and of an orphanage. Later it was the scene of Olympic tryouts and of a movie set.

A combination orphanage and reform school, the House of Refuge opened on the site in 1855. The Union Army confiscated some rooms in the institution for hospital space for convalescing Union soldiers wounded at the Siege of Vicksburg. After closing the orphanage, the Board of Children's Guardians gave the land to the St. Louis Parks Department in 1915.

The popularity of the pool at Fairground Park made clear the need for an open-air pool convenient to South Siders. Marquette swimming pool opened on July 8, 1916. Daily attendance that summer averaged fifteen hundred. The pool not only served generations of South Siders, but it also hosted the water polo tryouts for the 1948 U.S. Olympic team. In 1960, the pool was replaced with a new 165-foot-long L-shaped pool.

In 1921, crews of prisoners from the City Work House demolished the remaining orphanage buildings on the west half of the park to make way for tennis courts, trees, and athletic fields. Those fields became a film set for crews and actors recreating soccer games for the 2005 release *The Game of Their Lives*. The movie chronicled the United States team—with six St. Louisans—that defeated the favored English team in the 1950 World Cup.

Marquette Park
Founded: 1915
Size: 16 acres
Cost: Donated

BABY BOOM PARKS

The post–World War II baby boom spurred the postwar housing boom. Suddenly, on the southwest fringes of the city, bobcats and carpenters were turning the lots and blocks, which had been left vacant during the Great Depression, into vibrant neighborhoods. The city created two new parks that serve as extended backyards in these baby boomer neighborhoods—Tilles and Lindenwood parks.

Both parks host practices, games, and tournaments for the Catholic Youth Council, recreation programs funded by propositions, numerous parishes and clubs, and the Judge Dowd Soccer League. Their athletic fields and courts are in almost continual use from mid-April through mid-December.

Lindenwood Park was part of a Spanish land grant made to Charles Gratiot in 1798. The parkland forms a shallow, three-sided, shady valley facing Jamieson Avenue. With baseball, softball, and soccer fields; tennis and horseshoe courts; a playground; and a roller hockey rink, Lindenwood Park offers recreation for all ages.

Lindenwood Park
Founded: 1915
Size: 14 acres
Cost: $81,000

Tilles Park
Founded: 1957
Size: 29 acres
Cost: $380,000

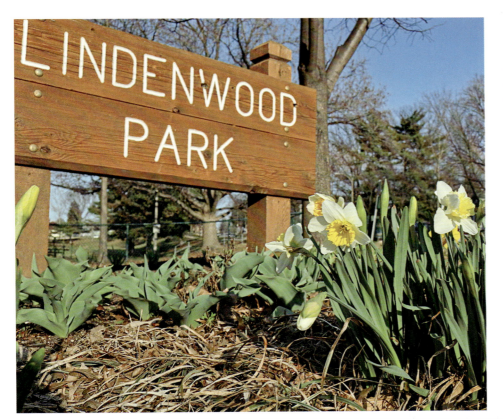

Tilles Park, facing the east side of Hampton Avenue, serves its 1950s vintage neighborhood with baseball, softball, and soccer fields; basketball, racquetball, tennis, and volleyball courts; a roller hockey rink; and playgrounds. The terrace near the Fyler Avenue border of the park features Frank Lloyd Wright–style stonework and rectangular flower beds that reflect the neighborhood's modern style.

The Campau subdivision, which was platted in 1952, forms the park's eastern border. The "Potter's Field," or city cemetery, occupied the ground opposite the park on Fyler since before the turn of the century. The bodies were moved about 1950 and the site developed as the 510-unit Hampton Gardens Apartments, which was completed in 1952.

The establishment of Tilles Park on Hampton is directly tied to the history of the park by the same name in St. Louis County. In 1932, Captain Tilles donated fifty-eight acres at McKnight and Litzinger roads for a city park in memory of his mother, Rosalie. The city was able to sell that park to the county system and use the money to buy the parkland on Hampton Avenue.

BERRA PARK

Founded: 1945
Size: 4.8 acres
Cost: $15,000

The base of every light standard, and even the drinking fountain, in Berra Park is painted red, white, and green to evoke the flag of Italy, announcing the Italian-American heritage of the surrounding neighborhood, the Hill. A huge bust of Louis G. (Midge) Berra greets visitors at the main entrance to the park, a flat, square acreage filled with ball fields and a playground. The park was renamed for Berra, St. Louis's first Italian-American to be elected to citywide office, in 1965. It is home to a meatball-eating contest and other festivities that celebrate Columbus Day.

THIS MEMORIAL IS DEDICATED TO THE MEMORY OF

LOUIS G. MIDGE BERRA

A DISTINGUISHED CITIZEN AND A SERVANT OF THE PEOPLE

1906 — 1964

CARONDELET LIONS PARK

Founded: 1929
Size: 1.7 acres
Cost: $15,458

Once the ball field for local Irish-American and German-American children, Carondelet Lions Park is now the front yard for the Temtor, an old Coca-Cola syrup plant that has been converted into loft-style apartments. The plant was built in 1919 for a fruit preserves company.

Irish St. Louisan and philanthropist Bryan Mullanphy purchased the parkland in 1843. He bequeathed the property to the Mullanphy Emigrant Relief Fund. Informally known as Mullanphy Park, it was renamed Carondelet Lions Park after the Lions Club of Carondelet worked with the city of St. Louis in grading, sodding, and installing playground equipment in 1963.

CHAIN OF ROCKS PARK

Founded: 1910
Size: 29.76 acres

The Water Department purchased this forested river bluff in 1893 to protect the healthful setting adjacent to the waterworks. An amusement park, located on top of the bluff, spurred use of public picnic grounds from 1927 to 1978. The new St. Louis Riverfront Trail connecting with Downtown St. Louis and the renovated multi-use Chain of Rocks Bridge is again increasing the park's popularity with bikers and walkers.

CHEROKEE PARK

Founded: 1924
Size: 8.9 acres
Cost: Purchased for $90,000

A private beer garden was operating on this acreage by the Civil War. Nearby Lemp Brewery then bought the garden and operated it as Lemp's Park. During Prohibition, the city used bond-issue money to buy the land and turn it into a public park. The State Highway Department cut off the corner of the park for the construction of Interstate 55.

COMPTON HILL RESERVOIR PARK

Founded: 1867
Size: 35.8 acres
Cost: $100,000

Following the Civil War, the city chose this acreage for a reservoir because it was the highest spot within the then city limits. The Water Department maintained the surrounding acreage as a park, so the trees and plant life would filter the air around the open reservoir. By the turn of the century, groves of oaks shaded the east side, and floral displays highlighted the west side. The 175-foot water tower was built in 1898 at a cost of $48,000. On August 6, 1961, the Water Department turned over the maintenance of the surrounding park to the Parks Department. The construction of I-44 encroached on the northern border of the thirty-five-acre park.

COLUMBUS SQUARE

Founded: 1908
Size: .45 acres, originally 2.16
Cost: $236,641

On July 17, 1914, Columbus Square was the site of the first "Municipal Movie" presented in a city park. The crowd of about three thousand included "mothers and babies, fathers and small boys, Italians, Greeks, Poles, Jews, Irish, Germans and two-generation Americans." The half-acre square, established in 1908, is surrounded by a new downtown neighborhood.

FOUNTAIN PARK

Founded: 1889
Size: 1.5 acres
Cost: Gift of John Lay

A statue of Dr. Martin Luther King Jr., by sculptor Rudolph Torrini, overlooks this small, oval park surrounded by handsome brick homes. The statue was unveiled in the park in 1978. The developer of Aubert Place reserved this green oval at the center of the subdivision before the Civil War. In 1889, the oval became a city park.

FOX PARK

Founded: 1917
Size: 2.69 acres
Cost: $85,000

The big-league-style scoreboard reigns over the outfield of the Police Athletic League ball field in Fox Park. Cardinals Care, the charitable arm of the St. Louis Cardinals, and the late Cardinal pitcher Darryl Kile funded the renovation of the ball field for use by the league and by neighborhood children. The park features a brick Italian, Romanesque-style shelter dating to the early twentieth century.

JACKSON PLACE

Founded: 1816
Size: 1.62 acres
Cost: Gift

Young evergreens ring little Jackson Park, the flat circle of ground facing I-70 that has a rich history. The founders of the town of North St. Louis, later annexed by the city of St. Louis, set aside the circle of land for public assembly and recreation. By the Gilded Age, an ornate, tiered, cast-iron fountain graced the center of the circle. Walks, benches, and substantial trees surrounded the fountain. As the neighborhood evolved into a crowded immigrant community, the circle became a busy playground. In 1902, three to four thousand people passed through the circle daily, many on their way to streetcar stops.

LUCAS GARDENS PARK

Founded: 1857
Size: 1.09 acres
Cost: Gift of James H. and Marie E. Lucas

With its prominent location, block-sized Lucas Park has experienced extreme ups and downs but has a bright future facing the grand new entrance of the Main Branch of the St. Louis Public Library.

The park, a sunken garden, had been the site of the brick home built by Judge John B. C. Lucas in 1820. His descendants gave the land to the city as a "public Promenade." The park's delightful, ornamental drinking fountain and park benches were sculpted in 1915. During most of the twentieth century the rectangular, sunken, formal gardens were a favorite spot to read a book just checked out from the adjacent library. The library piped light classical music into the park during lunch hours. During the 1980s, organizations from outlying areas began delivering homeless to the park, and left litter and debris as they used it as a distribution site for supplies for the homeless. With the renovation of nearby warehouses as lofts, new downtown residents spurred the creation of a dog park within Lucas Park. The park will continue to evolve when the renovated, Italian Renaissace-inspired library reopens with an atrium and elegant fountain looking onto the Lucas Garden.

MCDONALD PARK

Founded: 1928
Size: 3 acres
Cost: $12,650

McDonald Playground at Utah and Bent serves the Oak Hill neighborhood with its softball and soccer fields, spraypools, and playground. This park was one of many small parks that the city established so that no child would have to walk more than a half-mile to a playground.

MINNIE WOOD SQUARE

Founded: 1925
Size: 4.5 acres
Cost: Gift of Minnie Wood Estate

Ninety-year-old sycamores border Minnie Wood Memorial Square, with its busy athletic field. The tip of the wedge of parkland along South Broadway at Meramec Street was transferred from the Street Department to the Parks Department in 1910 and called the Meramec Triangle. In 1925, the estate of Mrs. Minnie Wood purchased the adjacent 4.5 acres and donated it to the city for a playground. Minnie was a German immigrant who married an English immigrant. Together, they ran a boarding house for milk wagon drivers. She received a substantial settlement in their separation, which paid for the park. In 1927, the city built the Mission Revival–style shelter and a wading pool.

ROBERT TERRY PARK

Founded: 1945
Size: 4 acres
Cost: $40,000

This park site was the grounds of the home of James Buchanan Eads, the premier nineteenth-century Mississippi River engineer and builder of the Eads Bridge. The city named the park for a neighborhood resident, Dr. Robert Terry. Terry was a leader in the conservation movement. A new neighborhood, the Gate District, is gradually growing up near Terry Park.

ST. LOUIS PLACE PARK

Founded: 1859
Size: 14.13 acres
Cost: Donated

A chain of four rectangular blocks that intersects St. Louis Avenue at 21st Street forms St. Louis Place Park. The original ten acres were donated to the city in 1850. Park records state the land was a "Gift of John Miller, et al." The southernmost block, south of Benton Street, had been the site of an earthen, wood-lined water reservoir from about 1850 to 1870. The weekend following Labor Day, polka music echoes through this park from the annual festival held at the adjacent Polish Falcons Hall.

SHERMAN PARK

Founded: 1917
Size: 22 acres
Cost: $196,560

*S*herman Park was the campus of Christian Brothers College, which burned in 1916. The site, facing Kingshighway, fit into the Kingshighway Plan of an emerald necklace of parks and boulevards circling the city. In 1917, the city purchased the property and converted the remaining school building into a community center. In 1959, a new recreation center was built facing Kingshighway.

SISTER MARIE CHARLES PARK

Founded: 1948
Size: Nearly one mile

*W*ith overlooks resting on the riverbank, this park at the foot of Chouteau's bluff and below Bellerive Park offers a rare opportunity to get close to the Mississippi River. This linear park provides walks between the limestone bluffs, the railroad tracks and the river. During high water, the barges rise to eye level with the walkways.

This section of riverbank was home to a Hooverville built during the Great Depression. Shanties raised on stilts stood on this site into the 1960s. Sister Marie Charles, director of Carondelet Community Betterment Federation Inc. and one of the Sisters of St. Joseph of Carondelet, lobbied for the creation of this riverside park.

SOUTH ST. LOUIS SQUARE

Founded: 1882
Size: 1.66 acres
Cost: Donated

South St. Louis Square hosts the annual Bastille Day celebration for its Carondelet neighborhood, which was an independent French village. Once a market square, the park has become a catch-all for remnants and symbols of its community's varied history. The brick store building in the park's northeast corner was constructed as a public market just before St. Louis annexed Carondelet in 1870. The historic stone house in the park's southeast corner was built by Bavarian immigrant Anton Schmitt in 1859. (This house was moved to the park in 1992.) In 2011, local business leaders installed a replica of a 32-pounder, Civil War–era naval cannon to recall that James B. Eads constructed Union ironclads in Carondelet.

SUBLETTE PARK

Founded: 1915
Size: 13.52 acres
Cost: From the Hospital Division

As children, big leaguers Joe Garagiola and Yogi Berra played baseball in Sublette Park. The triangular park had been the site of the Social Evil Hospital, later named the Female Hospital. The park occupies the highest point in the city.

TANDY PARK

Founded: 1918
Size: 5.6 acres
Cost: $102,380

The city purchased the acres at Pendleton and Cottage to create Tandy Park in the historic African-American neighborhood, the Ville. The park was named for Civil War veteran Captain Charlton H. Tandy, a pioneer in African-American education in Missouri.

During the 1920s, Tandy Field was home to four teams in the Colored Industrial League, including the Scullin Steel Mules and Pullman Shops Nine.

In an era of segregated playground programs, Tandy served African-American children along with three other playgrounds, Carr, Columbus, and Gamble. Together, their attendance for the summer of 1934 was 223,274.

YEATMAN SQUARE

Founded: 1906
Size: 3.4 acres
Cost: $40,000

Following World War II, thirty quonset huts were constructed on the site of Yeatman Playground to provide emergency housing for African-American veterans returning to over-crowded St. Louis. The land was eventually returned to park use, but gradually, many of the surrounding houses were abandoned.

"Make me a channel of your peace..."
The prayer of St. Francis

In memory of

Martie J. (Jay) Aboussie, Jr.

February 1, 1983 - May 3, 2006

enerations of civic leaders created scores of small parks so that squares of lawns and trees would be focal points of neighborhoods and all St. Louis children could walk easily to a playground. While not every such park has as distinctive a story as the featured parks, each one has provided health and happiness for St. Louis children over the decades. Some of the small parks that once served crowded neighborhoods are now underused, some are surrounded by vacant lots and empty buildings. However, as these parks were once lush centerpieces of community life, they can now spur neighborhood renaissances.

The city park system, in addition to the featured parks, includes:

Aboussie Park (.4 acres), Alaska Park (4.7 acres), Amberg Park (2.8 acres), Amherst Park (4.4 acres), Jet Banks Park (3.4 acres), Barrett Brothers Park (13 acres), Beckett Playground (3.3 acres), E. "Tink" Bradley Park (3.2 acres), Buder Playground (2.3 acres), Busche Park (6 acres), Carnegie Park (2 acres), Jordan Chambers Park (6 acres), Chouteau Park (1.2 acres), Desoto Park (17.3 acres), Dickman Park (5.21 acres), Dwight Davis Park (9.6 acres), Eads Park (4.2 acres), Fanetti Plaza (1.7 acres), Father Filipiac Park (4.3 acres), Fourteenth Street Mall (1.27 acres), Marie Fowler Park (.7 acres), Francis R. Slay Park (9 acres), Franz Park (4.7 acres), Greg Freeman Park (.9 acres), Freemont Park (2.3 acres), Gwen Giles Park (5.4 acres), Loretta Hall Park (2.3 acres), Hamilton Heights Park (1.3 acres), W.C. Handy Park (12 acres), Hickey Park (16 acres), Interco Plaza (.71 acres), Samuel Kennedy Park (1 acre), Kingsbury Square Park (.6 acres), Ray Leisure Park (7.3 acres), Phillip Lucier Park (3 acres), Mestres Park (3 acres), Minnesota & Hill Park (.5 acres), Murphy Park (10 acres), North Riverfront Park (250 acres, when combined with Chain of Rocks), Parkland Park (2.4 acres), Ivory Perry Park (11 acres), Ruth Porter Mall (8 acres), River des Peres Extension (11 acres), Rumbold Park (3 acres), Russell Park (1.1 acres), St. Marcus Park (26 acres), Norman Seay Park (3 acres), Strodtman Park (1.7 acres), Tambo Park (1 acre), Taylor Park (.3 acres), Tiffany Park (1.1 acres), Turner Playground (1.4 acres), Unity Park (2 acres), Vivian-Astra Park (1.1 acres), Walnut Park (2.3 acres), Washington Square (13.5 acres), and Windsor Park (3.3 acres).

In addition, the following parks—Adams Park, Baer Plaza, Blasé Park, Jefferson National Expansion Memorial Park, Kiel Triangle Park, and Leon Strauss Park—are operated by other civic and municipal entities or the federal government.

COUNTY PARKS

Esley Hamilton

Photography by Steve Tiemann

INTRODUCTION

While the city of St. Louis created an outstanding park system in the nineteenth century, little thought was given to parks in St. Louis County until after the World's Fair, and then the impetus came primarily from progressive city interests. The Civic League proposed a city-county "public reservation district" in 1907. They hired landscape architect George Kessler to design a comprehensive plan of parks and parkways that would link scenic areas throughout the region. Kessler had successfully created such an integrated network in Kansas City. His Outer Park plan here highlighted the bluffs above Columbia Bottoms, Spanish Lake, Charbonier Bluff west of Florissant, Creve Coeur Lake, the Meramec Highlands of western Kirkwood and the bottomland below them now in Fenton, and the Jefferson Barracks U.S. military reservation. Voters rejected the plan in 1910, and the Missouri Supreme Court ruled against the proposed regional district in 1913.

Florissant's Spanish Land Grant Park goes back to the founding of the community in 1786, when it was intended to be a marketplace and a site for the parish church. Bridgeton, another Spanish settlement, incorporated in 1843, followed by Florissant, Kirkwood, and Fenton, but they were surrounded by countryside and not in need of parks. University City, founded in 1906, was by contrast an extension of the fast-growing central city, and it seems to have been the first municipality to establish its own park system, beginning in 1920 with Lewis Park, the former backyard of the city's founder, E. G. Lewis. The Park Board worked with the School Board to purchase adjacent parcels, as at Flynn Park (1923) with Flynn Park School and Millar Park (1929) with Nathaniel Hawthorne School. Gradually,

A. P. Greensfelder (left) poses with Herman Barken in 1953.

other cities set aside their own parks. Clayton opened Shaw Park in 1937, and Webster Groves voted the funds for Blackburn Park in 1945.

The city of St. Louis made an effort in the 1930s to establish a regional park system on lands it owned in the county, using WPA and PWA funds from New Deal programs. C. A. ("Cap") Tilles, who had made his fortune through racetracks and off-track gambling, presented Tilles Park at McKnight and Litzsinger roads to the city of St. Louis in 1932. It remained a city park until 1957. Fort Belle Fontaine and the Buder property across from Valley Park were also intended to be city parks. The state of Missouri entered the park scene in 1934 when Jacob and Henry Babler gave over 2,100 acres in memory of their brother. It was developed through another New Deal program, the Civilian Conservation Corps.

The first park to be presented to the county government was Creve Coeur Park, dedicated in 1945 as a war memorial. Since the county had no parks department, Creve Coeur was managed by a board of trustees, for many years under the guidance of A. P. Greensfelder, a University City business-man who became a leading advocate of conservation and rational city and regional planning. When the Tyson Valley ammunition "dump" or storage facility was declared surplus by the federal government in 1947, the county was able to acquire a tract twice the size of Forest Park, but the Korean War a few years later required its return to the Department of Defense.

A new county charter replaced the old three-judge system in 1950 with a county superintendent (now called county executive) and county council. Article IV of the charter created a department of parks and recreation under a commissioner (later director). That same year, the county was able to acquire Sylvan Springs Park and the first part of Jefferson Barracks Park as surplus federal lands. West Tyson Park was reclaimed from the Tyson Valley site in 1955, and Lone Elk Park at the east end of that tract rejoined the park system in 1964 after a long struggle. The Parks and Recreation Advisory Board was set up in 1951.

County Supervisor Luman Matthews created the St. Louis County

Historic Buildings Commission in 1957 by executive order, confirmed by ordinance in 1982. The federal gift of the former ordnance section of Jefferson Barracks required the county to set up a museum telling the military history of the base, and Matthews asked the commission to help with that. The Powder Magazine Museum opened in 1960. The first chairman of the commission was Charles van Ravenswaay, then the director of the Missouri Historical Society. As editor of the *WPA Guide to Missouri* and a noted expert on Missouri history, van Ravenswaay saw the commission's potential and emphasized its role in identifying and preserving the county's historic resources. The Historic Preservation Commission (known to the staff as the HBC) thus became the earliest local government preservation body in the state.

Since its beginning, the park system has benefitted from the generosity of individuals who have donated both land and funds for facilities. Their stories are among the most interesting aspects of park history. Buder Park, for example, reflects the newspaper history of the region, as the Buder

Historic Buildings Commission, 1966

A steam locomotive along
Creve Coeur Lake

CREVE COEUR LAKE
MEMORIAL PARK

PRESENTED TO
ST. LOUIS COUNTY
1944
IN RECOGNITION OF THE SERVICES
SACRIFICES AND ACHIEVEMENTS
OF OUR ARMED FORCES

DEDICATED JUNE 3, 1945

COUNTY COURT
L. F. MATTHEWS, P.J.
A. V. BARTELSMEYER   A. V. SCHMID
BOARD OF PARK TRUSTEES
A. P. GREENSFELDER, CH.
J. E. AUCHLY   L. C. W. HECHT
M. C. FOGERTY   J. L. WERNER
C. J. MUCKERMAN

AMERICAN LEGION
10TH DISTRICT
DEPARTMENT OF MISSOURI

FOREVER TO REMEMBER"

family at one time owned both the *St. Louis Times* and the German-language *Westliche Post*. The park came to the county in 1954 through provisions in the will of Gustavus A. Buder Sr., who had first given the land in 1917 to the city of St. Louis.

John Allen Love founded Prudential Savings and Loan of St. Louis. His wife, Mary Potter Love, was perhaps better known than he, as the first local woman to head her own real estate company. They gave Love Park in 1959, naming the picnic shelters after two of their daughters: Mary, who married Frederick Lehmann III; and Cynthia, called "Muffin," who married Ben Roth. Another park using a family nickname is Suson, which was acquired in 1962 from Sidney Salomon Jr., the first owner of the St. Louis Blues hockey team. The name comes from his two children Susan and Sidney III, called "Sonny."

While on the subject of names, it should be noted that two park names are the result of misprints. Forrest Staley Park is named for Forest H. Staley (1885–1941), who supported the Boy Scout troop that uses this property. The court order transferring the property to the county in 1980 added the extra "r." Bella Fontaine Park results from a 1960 query from the parks director to the mayor of Bellefontaine Neighbors. He suggested that the park name be written as two words, as it was in the nineteenth century. His secretary, however, typed "*Bella*," the Italian word for "beautiful," instead of the French "*Belle*."

The Bissell House, near Bella Fontaine Park, was a gift beginning in 1960 from Janet Bissell Dimond, the great-granddaughter of General Daniel Bissell. (The home of the general's nephew Lewis Bissell in the Hyde Park neighborhood had been saved in 1958.) Restoration was led by HBC member Carolyn McDonnell (Mrs. William S. McDonnell), who at the same time was leading the restoration of the Thomas Sappington House, owned by the city of Crestwood but also supported by the HBC.

Another member of the HBC, Leicester Busch Faust, and his wife, Mary, gave one hundred acres for Faust Park in 1968, including Thornhill, the home of Missouri's second governor, Frederick Bates. Mary's bequest doubled the park in 1996 and included her own home and other noteworthy buildings. Leicester Faust was a grandson of Adolphus Busch of Anheuser-Busch and also of Tony Faust, the most famous restaurateur in St. Louis at the turn of the twentieth century. Norman Champ of the Champ Spring Company, along with his brother Joseph, gave the forty-nine-acre Champ Park in 1971, then joined the HBC two decades later.

Howard C. Ohlendorf's company made supplies for orthodontists. He and his wife, Irma, made many gifts to the park system, including part of Ohlendorf Park and the forty-six-acre Ohlendorf Park West on Hanna Road. They donated fountains for the lakes at Tilles and Queeny parks. Most importantly, they rescued the St. Louis Carousel from the old Forest Park Highlands Amusement Park in 1965 for Sylvan Springs Park, then fifteen years later contributed generously to its restoration at Faust Park.

Real estate broker Edwin F. Bright gave his nineteenth-century Brightfield

Ed Bright and Beulah

Leicester Busch Faust, his daughter Ann, and granddaughters

Dedication of Buder Park monument

Jeannette L. Windegger

John Allen Love and Wayne Kennedy

Henry and Matilda Laumeier

Farm complex south of Manchester in 1974. The park site remains undeveloped, but the barn and smokehouse are now part of the village at Faust Park. Bright became a local celebrity because of his mule Beulah, who was named World's Champion Riding Mule at a national show in 1971. Beulah and Bright were often featured in parades and represented Missouri national bicentennial events in 1976. Bright donated the equestrian shelter at Greensfelder Park, which he was proud to say was the only shelter in Missouri and probably in the nation named for a mule. He died in 1979, but Beulah survived in the care of County Parks until her death in 1998. She is also remembered at Greensfelder by a trail and a campsite.

Charles R. Skow, a mayor of Brentwood, was elected to the County Council in 1950 and became the first official park commissioner in 1957. A shelter at Tilles Park was named in his memory after he died unexpectedly in 1962 at the age of forty-nine. Skow was succeeded by Wayne C. Kennedy, the department's recreation supervisor who had won a national award from the National Recreation Association the previous year. Kennedy had been a teacher and administrator in the Mehlville (R-9) School District before becoming involved in recreation through leading a

grassroots effort to construct the R-9 Community Center. In nearly thirty years as director of parks and recreation, Kennedy brought the system to essentially its present size and configuration.

He paid for this expansion from about one thousand to over twelve thousand acres by continuing the bond issues that had been initiated by Greensfelder and Skow and by obtaining a wide variety of public and private grants. Bond issues passed in 1955 and 1959 permitted the development of several neighborhood sites. The bond issue of 1969 provided $25 million for the purchase of Queeny Park, the development of north, south, and west recreation complexes, and much else. Another bond issue in 1977 permitted the acquisition of McDonnell and St. Vincent Park, along with other sites, while the 1986 bond issue provided funds for the Fountain Lake sports complex at Bella Fontaine, the community center at St. Vincent, a memorial to military veterans at Jefferson Barracks, and other projects.

Funds from bond issues were often used to match federal grants, especially from the Interior Department's Land and Water Conservation Fund, which is generated by revenues from leases for offshore oil and

St. Louis County Parks 87

gas drilling. Parklands acquired or developed with these funds cannot be diverted to other uses unless replaced in kind. Bond issue funds were also matched by private foundations. A. P. Greensfelder's generosity continued after his death in 1955 through foundations he organized. One of them, the St. Louis Regional Planning and Construction, gave Greensfelder Park in 1963, while the Albert P. Greensfelder Foundation funded the Greensfelder Recreation Complex in Queeny Park.

Groups of citizens coming together to support one particular park have become increasingly important. The Transport Museum Association (TMA) has aided the Museum of Transportation since 1948. Laumeier Sculpture Park has its own board and staff. Several groups operate under the umbrella of the Historic Sites Foundation of St. Louis County, a charitable organization whose only members are its board of three people. One such, the Friends of the Carousel, has expanded it focus to become the Faust

The Carousel Building at Faust Park

Cultural Heritage Foundation. The Friends of Jefferson Barracks is another. The Open Space Council was organized in 1965 as an independent organization with many conservation interests, but it has often assisted the county, most critically in 1968 when they raised the matching funds to the rescue of the Nims Estate, Bee Tree Farm, now Bee Tree Park. The house designed by Frank Lloyd Wright for Ruth & Russell Kraus was saved in 2001 after a six-year campaign by citizens, and they now administer the facility as the Frank Lloyd Wright House in Ebsworth Park.

Mr. Kennedy, as he was called by staff, gained a reputation for his ability to awaken the generosity of donors. In response to his efforts, for example, Matilda Laumeier (called "Pink" by the family) bequeathed her estate in Sunset Hills in memory of her husband, Henry. Ethel Queeny, who with her husband, Edgar, had sold their large estate near Town and

Country to developers, later changed her mind and contributed over a million dollars to its development as a park. Cap Tilles had given Jeanette L. Windegger a life tenancy in his house at Tilles Park, and she remained there from 1932 until the late 1970s, when she decided to move out so that the beautiful Windegger Shelter could be built on the site. A few of Kennedy's efforts did not end as hoped, however. Delbert Wenzlick died of a heart attack in 1979 while discussing the possible donation of his White Haven estate. Lee Hunter of Hunter Engineering talked about bequeathing his Hunter Farm estate on Ladue Road but failed to make any provisions before his death in 1986.

Kennedy also knew how to work with companies that were extracting sand and gravel from along the Meramec River. Winter Brothers Material Company donated George Winter Park near Fenton in 1971 and Robert

Jarville House at Queeny Park

Golden Eagle River Museum, a volunteer organization dedicated to preserving riverboat lore, occupied the Nims Mansion at Bee Tree Park until 2004 when it distributed its collections to other institutions. The National Civilian Conservation Corps Alumni Association restored a building at Jefferson Barracks originally built in 1898 as quarters for two officers but then moved to Virginia in 2008. The park system's newest museum is the Missouri Civil War Museum, whose organization worked for ten years to restore the old Post Exchange and Gymnasium Building at Jefferson Barracks.

The range of activities in the parks reflects Mr. Kennedy's philosophy. He argued that in a culture as diverse as ours nothing was of interest to everyone but that everyone was interested in something. The broader the range of opportunities the parks could provide, the richer the experience for everyone. In practice this meant that park management had to remain alert to changing interests. The mini-bike park at Antire Park and the go-kart track at Widman Park have gone away, while model planes are still being flown at Buder Park and Frisbee golf is gaining in popularity at Jefferson Barracks. Special events have also varied over the years, and some that once attracted thousands are now history. The Meramec River Raft Race was not really a race but a slow progression down the Meramec River from Unger to Winter Park, with prizes given for the most interestingly decorated vessels. The Haunted Forest was a pre-Halloween event that led hayrides past a series of scary features at Tilles Park. Mud Mania was an obstacle course for children that was guaranteed to result in the dirtiest possible participant.

Winter, an undeveloped site on the opposite side of the river, in 1983. Simpson Sand and Gravel Company made a partial donation of the Simpson Park site in 1976. The excavations these companies made have been transformed into picturesque water features.

By the late 1960s, the county had several parks that might be considered cultural attractions, including Bissell House, the museum at Jefferson Barracks, and the children's farm at Suson. Laumeier Park, originally intended to be a nature study area, became a sculpture park in 1976, one of the first in the nation. The Museum of Transportation became a county park in 1979. Founded in 1944, it had assembled nationally significant collections that exceeded its ability to maintain. A more controversial museum appeared in 1985 when the Museum of the Dog moved from New York City to the historic Jarville House in Queeny Park. Since 1995, it has been affiliated with the American Kennel Club. The restored St. Louis Carousel opened in a climate-controlled building at Faust Park in 1987, emphasizing its status as a valuable work of American art.

Robert J. Hall, who became director of parks in 1995, was particularly attuned to changing park interests after twenty-two years managing the recreation division of the department. He was particularly aware of the intertwined interests in walking, hiking, and biking and in protecting scenic riverways. The Meramec River Recreation Association, active since 1972, was already a model of how intergovernmental cooperation can safeguard such resources, and the county's contribution included the Walston Chubb Trail on the south bank of the river and the Al Foster

Trail on the north bank. The Danforth Foundation's "St. Louis 2004" initiative presented an opportunity to create a regional park and recreation district for these purposes. Hall resigned from the county in 1999 to lead this effort, which culminated in November 2000 with the passage of Proposition C. It created the Great Rivers Greenway District, a new unit of government in St. Charles County and St. Louis City and County with its own dedicated sales tax channeling funds to park, trail, and riverway projects at the regional, county, and city levels.

While parks consistently receive the greatest popular support of any county functions, relations between the department and the public have not always been happy. One particular source of antagonism has been the conflict over how or whether to develop Queeny Park. After battles in the 1960s and 1970s, this culminated in 1986 with a referendum to limit development in five so-called Heritage Parks: Cliff Cave, Greensfelder, Pelican Island, Queeny, and St. Stanislaus. Partly as a result of that, the county gave Pelican Island to the Missouri Department of Conservation and turned over St. Stanislaus on a long-term lease.

Other park properties have been transferred to other jurisdictions over the years. As the county's emphasis has shifted from small neighborhood playgrounds to multiuse regional parks, and as more cities have created their own park systems, fifteen parks have been turned over to local jurisdictions. White Haven, saved from demolition in 1986 by a joint effort of the county and the Missouri Department of Natural Resources, became Ulysses S. Grant National Historic Site, a unit of the National Park Service, in 1990. Only a few developed parks have been lost: Grandview in Sunset Hills was taken in 1962 by Interstate 270. Airport expansion eliminated Fairmount playground. The Page Avenue Extension took about about forty acres of Creve Coeur Park, but federal-highway and open-space regulations required its replacement with more than one

Robert J. Hall

thousand acres of new parkland, making Creve Coeur the largest park in the system.

After half a century of almost uninterrupted growth, the county park system found itself increasingly challenged as it entered the twenty-first century. Voters narrowly rejected a 2004 proposal to establish a dedicated sales for county parks. The next year cuts to the park budget nearly eliminated history programs in the parks and would have closed the museums at Jefferson Barracks had not the Friends of JB agreed to staff them with volunteers. Since then park budgets have been in survival mode, buoyed only by funds from the regional park tax that permit playground and trail improvements to continue. The budget proposed for 2012 initially called for the permanent closure of twenty-three parks. As passed, the budget keeps these parks open but cuts nearly 14 percent of the department's funding. The principle that parkland should be inviolable is being challenged, as a 911 telephone facility is built in Ohlendorf West and half of Sylvan Springs Park is sold to Jefferson Barracks National Cemetery. The County Department of Highways plans to run the Northwest Parkway across St. Stanislaus Park and Charbonier Bluff (still not secure after a century), while the South County Connector will go through the River des Peres Parkway. The need for the public to defend the county's cherished legacy of parks has never been greater.

Aerial photograph of Jefferson Barracks

CREVE COEUR PARK

Creve Coeur Park is St. Louis County's first, largest, and busiest park, with over a million visitors annually. The lake was once a bend in the Missouri River. A second lake silted up early in the last century, and siltation reduced the big lake to an average depth of only eighteen inches before it was rescued by a major dredging operation from 1974 to 1981.

French settlers were calling the lake "Creve Coeur" before 1800. The phrase means "broken heart" and describes a great grief, sorrow, or affliction. What it refers to here is unknown. It could refer to several places or families in France, a fort in Illinois, or even a breed of chicken but certainly not the spurious nineteenth-century tale of an Indian maiden.

The lake became a resort area in the nineteenth century. Railroad lines were extended by the Missouri Pacific in 1881 and the rival Katy in 1886. Hotels, dance pavilions, and boat houses were built, and in 1889 Jacob Studt offered grounds and a subsidy for the annual county fair. It was held here for about thirty years. The outline of the racetrack used then can still be discerned. A streetcar line opened from the Delmar Loop in 1899, and the brick electric station remains in the upper park. That was also the site of a large amusement park known as Electric Park, which featured a 255-foot observation tower moved from the 1904 World's Fair. The lake declined in the 1920s as gangsters began to frequent the clubs along the lakefront and a poor residential subdivision was developed.

Creve Coeur Park
Founded: 1945
Size: 2,114 acres

A revival began in 1945, when a group of citizens led by A. P. Greensfelder donated four hundred acres to the county as a war memorial. The county then lacked a parks department, so a special administrative board was set up. The 1969 bond issue permitted the county to purchase all the land surrounding the lake, including the old subdivision with about 150 cottages.

The extension of Page Avenue across the south end of the lake in the 1990s controversially took 25.8 acres of parkland. In return, the park gained 1,005.8 acres west of the lake as well as many improvements, including trails, soccer fields, and a restaurant. Mallard Lake has been created to help control siltation, and five hundred acres on the site of the Upper Lake are being returned to wetland.

FAUST PARK

On its relatively small two hundred acres, Faust Park concentrates some of the most fascinating historical sites and busiest recreational attractions in the metropolitan area. The park began as a gift from Leicester Busch Faust and his wife, Mary, in 1968 and was doubled in size by a bequest from Mary Faust in 1996.

The land was part of the Thornhill estate acquired by Frederick Bates (1777–1825) in 1808 and 1809. Bates had come from Virginia at the request of Thomas Jefferson to be secretary for the Upper Louisiana Territory. He built his two-story timber-frame house about 1818 for his mother and siblings, marrying seventeen-year-old Nancy Opie Ball the next year. Bates succeeded Missouri's first governor Alexander McNair in 1824, but he died the following year at the age of forty-eight. He is buried in the family plot behind the house.

The Thornhill complex, including the main house, the two barns, granary, and other outbuildings, was listed in the National Register of Historic Places in 1974. Architect Richard Bliss restored the house, and it opened for tours in 1990. The peach orchard and log distillery building reflect the farm's original cash crop, peach brandy.

The St. Louis Carousel opened at Faust Park in 1987. It was created by the Gustav Dentzel Company of Philadelphia about 1920 and erected at Forest Park Highlands Amusement Park in 1929 with sixty-four hand-carved animals and two chariots. Howard Ohlendorf donated the carousel to St. Louis County in 1965.

Faust Park
Founded: 1967
Size: 197.39 acres

First used outdoors at Sylvan Springs Park, it reopened in its own building on May 9, 1987, following a privately funded restoration. That event was celebrated by the first St. Louis performance of Circus Flora, which has since become a St. Louis fixture.

The village of historic buildings in the park began in 1986 and has now grown to four residences, the Alt School, and nine outbuildings. Miles Seed Carriage House, now the Visitors Center, came from Jennings. An agreement to move the Spanish Lake Blacksmith Shop from Bellefontaine Road was reached in 2011.

The Fausts' own residence was built in 1919 to Pueblo Revival designs by St. Louis architect Tom P. Barnett. He also designed the secondary residence and a dovecot. Maritz, Young & Dusard enlarged the house in 1935–36 and added the chateau-like garage. The unique 1925 barn was the first building in the region to use the lamella truss structural system.

The Sophia M. Sachs Butterfly House and Education Center, designed by Christner Inc., opened in 1998 and became a division of the Missouri Botanical Garden in 2001. The site includes an outdoor butterfly garden and two large sculptures by St. Louisan Robert Cassilly.

The county's largest playground opened at Faust in 2006. ADA-accessible, it has continued to attract record numbers of users.

FORT BELLE FONTAINE

Connecticut native Daniel Bissell (1768-1833) came to St. Louis in 1808 when he was appointed commanding officer of Fort Belle Fontaine by Thomas Jefferson. By the time he departed for active duty in the War of 1812, Bissell had decided to settle here. He assembled an estate of nearly 2,300 acres, which he called Franklinville Farm. He may have started his Federal-style house in 1812, and construction continued until about 1819, creating an unusual L-shaped floorplan with two lobbies. General Bissell returned here in 1821 when he retired. About 1890 his grandson replaced the old stone kitchen with a two-story frame wing.

Five generations of Bissells resided here. Great-granddaughter Janet Bissell Dimond gave the nine remaining acres to the county between 1960 and 1964. Architect Gerhardt Kramer then restored the house, which was furnished with the assistance of St. Louis County Historic Buildings Commission member Carolyn McDonnell. It now reflects life during the first three generations of Bissells. The house was listed in the National Register of Historic Places in 1978.

County Parks now also owns the site of Fort Belle Fontaine overlooking the Missouri River at the mouth of Coldwater Creek, a park with outstanding scenic value as well as historic interest. Fort Belle Fontaine was established in 1805 as the first U.S. military installation west of the Mississippi River. The Lewis and Clark expedition camped here in 1806 on the last night of their epic journey, and the National Park Service has erected signs in the park commemorating that event. General Bissell moved the fort from the bank of the river to the top of the bluff after 1808. With the departure of the army for Jefferson Barracks in 1826, the fort disappeared.

Fort Belle Fontaine
Bissell Park
Founded: 1985
Size: 293.17 acres

The city of St. Louis acquired the site in 1913 for a juvenile rehabilitation facility called Bellefontaine Farm, later the Missouri Hills Home for Boys. The city developed the area along the river for use as a city park in the late 1930s, using WPA funds. This was part of the same effort that developed Tilles Park. Some remains are still visible, notably the monumental stone staircase descending from the bluff to the river.

The city sold a large portion of the Missouri Hills Home to the county in 1985, retaining the juvenile home buildings at the center of the site. The state of Missouri acquired that core in 1988, and the Division of Youth Services now operates it as the Fort Bellefontaine Campus.

GREENSFELDER PARK

Greensfelder Park forms the heart of a West County greenbelt that includes Camp Wyman, the Missouri Conservation Department's Rockwood Reservation and Rockwood Range, and Babler State Park. Much of this land was first assembled in the 1850s by William T. Christy and Robert K. Woods of Woods, Christy & Co., a dry goods company in downtown St. Louis. Woods and Christy formed a lumber company that logged the area. The property later passed to Christy's son Calvin M. Christy, who extracted the clay and other minerals on the property for his Christy Fire Clay Company, organized in 1881. Christy sold to Charles Evans in 1893, and Evans is said to have offered a three hundred-acre tract to the city of St. Louis for use as a park. To enhance the site, a dam was constructed in 1895 on the property's main tributary, but it washed away during the spring rains of 1896.

Mining continued on the property under the Cobb, Wright and Case Mining Company, which went bankrupt in 1938. Missouri's Conservation Commission then acquired part of the former Christy property for Rockwoods Reservation but omitted the park's later site. It suffered from periodic logging operations, intense grazing from the nearby Allenton stockyards, and fire. The last severe forest fire occurred on Easter Sunday, 1941.

The trustees of the St. Louis Regional Planning and Construction Foundation donated the park to St. Louis County in 1963. The foundation had been established in 1939 by A. P. Greensfelder (1879–1955), civic leader and chairman of the board of the Fruin-Colnon Construction Company. Albert Preston

A.P. Greensfelder Park
Founded: 1963
Size: 1,583.06 acres

Greensfelder had been the primary force behind the creation of Creve Coeur Park and became chairman of the county's first Parks Advisory Board. He intended the foundation to provide financial assistance to public improvements, civic projects, and engineering programs, especially education and research.

Originally called Rockwood Park, the park was officially renamed in September 1965. The first phase of construction began the next year. Another major development, involving picnic areas, the visitor center, the equestrian areas, and a new barn, was dedicated in 1973. The Muckerman

Shelter was completed in November 1981. In 1994, Sonya Glassberg dedicated the Myron Glassberg Pavilion in memory of her husband, who had been the nephew and ward of Mr. Greensfelder's wife, Blanche. The pavilion replaced a family picnic shelter that had formerly been in the park.

JEFFERSON BARRACKS

The U.S. War Department acquired the 1,700-acre Jefferson Barracks Military Reservation in 1826 and deactivated the army post in 1946. The Veterans Hospital and National Cemetery still occupy parts of the site, while the main parade ground with its historic buildings from the 1890s is controlled by the National Guard. The oldest surviving buildings date to the 1850s and are found in the northernmost 425 acres, now Jefferson Barracks Park, while the most historic landscape is protected by the smaller Sylvan Springs Park. The county acquired both from the General Services Administration immediately after the Parks Department was created in 1950.

Jefferson Barracks was founded six days after the death of Thomas Jefferson and in the following decades became an important staging center during wars and operations in the West. More than two hundred men who became Union and Confederate generals served here before the Civil War, including Grant and Lee. During that war, vast temporary hospitals at Jefferson Barracks treated the wounded from both sides. Park historian Marc Kollbaum has been telling this important story in his series of books, *Gateway to the West, The History of Jefferson Barracks*, for sale through the Friends of Jefferson Barracks.

In 1850 the St. Louis Arsenal opened a branch at the Barracks, intended to reduce the risk of explosion at its base in the Soulard neighborhood. The stone Laborer's House and Old Ordnance Room were built the following year, and the sturdy Powder Magazine followed in 1857. The county opened the Powder Magazine Museum in 1960 to document the history of the Barracks. The Old Ordnance Room houses changing exhibitions. Through the efforts of the Friends of Jefferson Barracks, the 1870 barn was restored and reconstructed in 2003 as a visitors and

A GRATEFUL NATION HONORS THE G.I.'S
THAT SAVED FREEDOM IN EUROPE
AND IN THE PACIFIC ISLANDS
DURING WORLD WAR II
DECEMBER 7, 1941 – AUGUST 15, 1945

"DUTY, HONOR, COUNTRY"
WE SHALL NEVER FORGET THE
SACRIFICES AND THEIR UNDAUNTED COURAGE
IN THE GREATEST BATTLE EVER FOUGHT
BY THE UNITED STATES ARMY

INFANTRY DIVISIONS				COMBAT ENGINEERS	
1ST	28TH	79TH	97TH	9TH	207TH
2ND	29TH	80TH	99TH	35TH	246TH
3RD	30TH	82ND ABN	100TH	49TH	248TH
4TH	35TH	83RD	101ST ABN	61ST	254TH
5TH	36TH	84TH	102ND	145TH	303RD
8TH	42ND	87TH	103RD	148TH	1137TH
9TH	44TH	90TH	104TH	158TH	1251ST
17TH ABN	75TH	94TH	106TH	168TH	1340TH
26TH	78TH	95TH			

FIELD ARTILLERY				ARMORED DIVISIONS	
12TH	333RD	110TH	467TH	2ND	11TH
17TH	549TH	135TH	468TH	3RD	14TH
174TH	691ST	197TH	555TH	4TH	2ND CAV
183RD	730TH	397TH	601ST	5TH	
194TH	755TH	438TH	777TH	6TH	CAVALRY
215TH	949TH	440TH	791ST	7TH	CAVALRY
220TH	965TH	452ND	839TH	8TH	5TH RANGERS
275TH	980TH			9TH	
285TH	995TH			10TH	

AAA AW BATTALIONS

1ST U.S. ARMY
3RD U.S. ARMY
8TH U.S. AIRFORCE
9TH U.S. AIRFORCE

AMERICAN LOSSES WERE:
19,485 KILLED
15,360 CAPTURED
45,155 WOUNDED

Jefferson Barracks
Founded: 1950
Size: 424.95 acres

education center, including a shop. The park also features the Veterans Memorial, an amphitheater designed in 1990 by Team Four Architects. The three-mile Dennis Schick Trail opened in 1995.

The Missouri Civil War Museum and the Southwestern Bell Pioneers have restored buildings facing the parade ground, and a museum dedicated to prisoners of war and those missing in action (POW-MIA) is planned.

Sylvan Springs Park was created by the army, beginning in 1939, when the 6th Infantry created a stone "beverage garden" around the springs. The USO hosted many shows there during World War II, with major entertainers such as Jeanette MacDonald and Judy Garland. After 1954 Sylvan Springs drew crowds with carnival rides in the spring. A skateboard park opened in 2007, designed by staff landscape architect Chris Ludwig and skateboarders themselves.

LAUMEIER PARK

*N*ow a sculpture park with a national reputation, Henry H. Laumeier Park was originally a country estate, one of a group of such estates created by business leaders, mostly of German origin, moving out along Watson and Gravois roads from the Compton Heights neighborhood of south St. Louis. Roland L. Kahle, built a house in 1917 on Rott Road next to his brother's new home. The Kahles Ringen Stove Company became part of the American Stove Company, maker of Magic Chef stoves. The architect, Ernst Janssen, was known for his large Compton Heights mansion. Here, he created a glorified stone bungalow with matching garage and gatehouse.

Henry H. Laumeier (1876–1959), a real estate investor from the same neighborhood as Kahle, purchased the estate in 1936. He married Matilda Cramer in 1941, and they expanded the Rott Road property to seventy-two acres. Matilda Laumeier met Wayne C. Kennedy, county parks director, in 1963 and discussed her desire for a park that would retain the landscape and not redevelop it with playing fields. She bequeathed the property to the county in 1968, including a gift of $25,000 toward to cost of development.

At first intended as a nature study center, Laumeier Park was transformed in 1975 by the offer made by St. Louis sculptor Ernest Trova to make a gift of forty of his own sculptures as the nucleus of a sculpture park and gallery. At that time, only a few such parks existed in the world, and in this country only the Storm King Center in New York had a similar mission.

Henry H. Laumeier Park
Founded: 1968
Size: 94.16 acres

With the Trova gift installed, the park reopened in 1976. Over the years, many sculptures have been installed temporarily, from months to years, making the park a constantly changing spectacle. Some were greeted by the public with dismay at first, but over the years appreciation has grown, aided by the park's education program. Alexander Liberman's enormous metal abstraction, "The Way," was once featured on the cover of the telephone book.

A group of friends purchased about twenty acres on the east boundary of the park in 1981 and held it for several years until the county could reimburse them. This woods has become the home for several large works commissioned specifically for the land from artists Jackie Ferrara, Mary Miss, Beverly Pepper, and others. Another site-specific commission by Richard Fleischner crosses Rott Road to include stone constructions on the north side. Gallery exhibitions in the house are frequent, and special events such as the juried art fair held on Mother's Day weekend have become traditions.

MUSEUM OF TRANSPORTATION

A group of people headed by Dr. John Roberts founded the National Museum of Transport in 1944. Dedicated to preserving landmarks of our transportation past, they made a mule-driven streetcar named "Bellefontaine #33" their first acquisition. In 1948 they incorporated as the Transport Museum Association (TMA) as a nonprofit organization. They were able to purchase a site for the museum that was itself historic, immediately adjacent to the historic Barrett Station. It includes one of the two Barretts Tunnels, the first railroad tunnels to be built west of the Mississippi River and the only remaining structures associated with the original Pacific Railroad in Missouri. They were constructed from 1851 to 1853 by James P. Kirkwood (for whom the city is named) and were listed in the National Register of Historic Places in 1978.

From streetcars and other public transport, the association expanded its collecting to include all types of rail vehicles, as well as selected automobiles. Caring for a giant locomotive that is standing out in the weather year-round is a costly business, and maintenance needs gradually overwhelmed the association. Parks Director Wayne C. Kennedy saw the need and recognized the potential prestige of keeping a nationally significant collection of this sort in the county, and in 1979 he arranged for the County Parks Department to assume operation of the museum on a lease basis. After five successful years, the county officially accepted the museum in 1984 as a gift from the founders.

In the years since, shelters have been built to protect the outside rail stock. Fifty percent of the museum's locomotives are one-of-a-kind or sole survivors. The Earl C. Lindbergh Automobile Center displays cars ranging from a 1901 St. Louis Motor Carriage Company vehicle, the oldest surviving, to Bobby Darin's 1960 Dream Car, along with a façade from the Coral Court Motel, a Route 66 landmark. Other collections include carriages and aircraft. The museum houses a nationally acclaimed research library, which contains a collection of transportation-related memorabilia and documents used by scholars both locally and nationally.

Although not as well known to the St. Louis public as it should be, the museum is recognized by experts as one of the largest and best collections of transportation vehicles in the world. The county, in partnership with the TMA, continues its efforts to improve the facilities and grounds, and construction of a new visitors center designed by Fox Architects Inc. opened in 2012.

QUEENY PARK

*Q*ueeny Park was once part of the estate of the late Mr. and Mrs. Edgar M. Queeny. Edgar Queeny was the former president and chairman of the board of Monsanto Chemical Company, which was founded by his father. The history of the land, however, traces much further back than the Queenys.

The Jarville House is, after the Hanley House in Clayton, the most imposing example of the Greek Revival style to survive in St. Louis County, and its comparative modesty suggests the distinction between what was thought proper for city and country. St. Louis was at the time a stronghold of the Greek Revival, the surviving example of which (the Courthouse, the old Cathedral, and the Chatillon-DeMenil House) only suggest the extent and splendor of the style as it was seen here. Jarville, at 1723 Mason Road, was built about 1854 by Hyacinth Renard. It was renovated by architect William Crowell of the firm of Mauran, Russell & Crowell following the Queenys' acquisition of it in 1931. The house was listed in the National Register of Historic Places in 1984. It currently houses the Museum of the Dog. A second historic house on the property is the Henry Weidman House off Weidman Road. It is customarily leased to park employees.

The Queenys sold their property to the American Investment Company Realty Corporation in 1964, giving the proceeds to Barnes Hospital. St. Louis County purchased the property from the American Investment Company in March 1970 for $3,310,000 from 1969 bond issue funds. Ethel Queeny contributed $1 million toward the completion of the family recreation complex. Edward Greensfelder, who represents the Albert P. Greensfelder Foundation, also donated $1 million for the project, along with an additional $50,000 for landscaping.

Sverdrup and Parcel & Associates Inc. served as architect for Greensfelder Memorial Complex, which began construction in June 1972 and was dedicated in September 1974. The main building houses a regulation-size ice-skating rink, skate rental and sharpening, concession area. and lockers. The main structure is also a multi-purpose building with 22,500 square feet that can accommodate special events. The original tent structure—completed in August of 1978, designed by Jones/Mayer & Associates Inc.—covered 14,000 square feet. The tensile cover was designed and assembled by Birdair Structures Inc. of Buffalo, New York. In June 1994, the tent was replaced by a pre-engineered metal canopy. Funds were contributed from Midwest Sport Hockey Inc. and Perry Turnbull, a former St. Louis Blues hockey player. This facility was enclosed in 1998 with private funding.

SPANISH LAKE PARK

*A*long with Creve Coeur Lake, the county's first park, and Charbonier Bluff, which still remains in private ownership, Spanish Lake has the longest history as a natural feature admired for its scenic beauty and recreational potential. Unlike Creve Coeur Lake, Spanish Lake was created not by shifting river channels but by the geology of the region. Depressions or sinkholes are caused by the collapse of the underlying limestone from groundwater erosion. Most sinkholes drain naturally, but if they become plugged, a pond results. Sunfish Lake, the second lake in this park, appeared in just this way in July 1942 when Ben Ruthmann found that his tomato field had been inundated.

Spanish Lake has been known as a beauty spot since colonial times, but it remained in private ownership until St. Louis County acquired it in 1971 with a federal grant and funds from the 1969 bond issue.

In the 1770s, Spanish troops were reportedly stationed at the temporary fort near the mouth of the Missouri River. Zenon Trudeau also had a country retreat at the lake. Records from 1809 show that the first to legally claim the northwest part of the lake was John Lard, whose son was the first owner of the nearby Fort Belle Fontaine site. The southeast part of the lake was claimed by Jacques St. Vrain, who had already purchased the site from the widow Rigoche. Through the rest of that century the lake was owned by prominent non-residents such as John O'Fallon, but in 1897 the Spanish Lake Park subdivision was platted by developers. Fortunately for posterity, it was not successful, but later subdivisions threatened the lake right up to the time the county intervened. Even today a significant tract of subdivided but undeveloped land remains immediately southeast of the park.

Spanish Lake Park
Founded: 1969
Size: 241.64 acres

Since its opening, the park has received several improvements. Fourteen acres were added in 1986, and the large Manny Broadway Shelter was built at an elevated point on the east side of the lake. The lake was dredged in the 1990s and is now managed by the Missouri Department of Conservation under the Community Assistance Program. The Cardinal Care Program of the baseball Cardinals constructed "Spirit Field," an accessible baseball field suitable for use by players in wheelchairs and others with disabilities.

TILLES PARK

$\mathcal{C}$. Andrew Tilles (1865–1951), called "Cap" by all, returned from Fort Smith, Arkansas, in 1876 to his native St. Louis, where he and his business partner Sam Adler parlayed a cigar store into the ownership of the South Side Race Track, later the site of McKinley High School. By 1906, Tilles, Adler, and Louis A. Cella were said to control more than half the racetracks in the country, including Little Rock, Hot Springs, Memphis, Detroit, Cincinnati, and Louisville. When Missouri outlawed horse-race betting that year, Tilles made even more by redeveloping his Delmar Race Track site in the present University City Loop.

Tilles acquired this park site in 1912 and created an estate he called "Rest Haven." He deeded it in 1932 to the city of St. Louis, specifying that it be named "Rosalie Tilles Children's Playground and Park" in honor of his mother and that it be open to persons regardless of race or creed. He reserved his modest home and the surrounding 7.67 acres for his lifetime and that of his housekeeper, Jeanette Windegger. He gave another park to the city of Fort Smith in memory of his father.

Works Progress Administration (WPA) projects in 1936 and 1937 created the stone entrance pylons, picnic shelters, and comfort stations, all designed by Louis Baylor Pendleton (1875–1964). He moved the iron fence at the main entrance from Hyde Park in North St. Louis. Tilles Park remains one the finest New Deal projects in the county.

When the county bought the park in 1957, the city used the proceeds to create a new twenty-nine-acre Rosalie Tilles Park on Hampton Avenue at Fyler. After County Park Commissioner Charles Skow died in 1962, an attempt was made to rename the county park for him, but in the end a new picnic shelter sufficed.

Another new shelter was named for Jeanette Windegger after she released her rights to the 7.67 acres in 1975. She devoted her remaining years to charitable works, dying in 1991 at the age of ninety-seven.

The St. Louis Children's Hospital Accessible Playground opened in 2006. Designed by SWT Design with staff landscape architect Mike Flad, it accommodates children with an unusually wide range of disabilities and has become one of the most popular attractions in the park system. Another popular annual attraction is Winter Wonderland, which swathes the park in lights through the month of December.

BEE TREE PARK

*L*ocated near the far southeast corner of St. Louis County, with sweeping views of the Mississippi River, Bee Tree Park was once remote, but today development extends right up to the entrance. Bee Tree was originally created as a private estate by Eugene Nims (1865–1954), president of Southwestern Bell Telephone Company. Nims had started a telephone company in Oklahoma in 1896. Its thirty-six miles of wire eventually grew into Southwestern Bell. Nims became president in 1919 and built the Southwestern Bell Building at 1010 Pine Street in 1924. He and his wife, the unusually named Lotawana Flateau Nims (called "Miss Molly" by her friends) lived in Portland Place and had a summer home in Woods Hole, Massachusetts, but they added the magnificent Tudor Revival house at Bee Tree Farm to their collection in 1929 and used it as a weekend retreat. The house is characteristic of the picturesque and finely crafted designs of Maritz & Young, the foremost St. Louis residential architects of the era.

After Mrs. Nims died in 1966, development threatened the 192-acre site. The Open Space Foundation, led by Lindell Gordon and R. Walston Chubb, was able to raise $197,000, which matched federal funds to enable the county to purchase the property in 1968. Gordon, a trust officer of the Mississippi Valley Trust Company, was fatally ill at the time, and after his death the park created a garden and fountain in his memory. The fountain sculpture represents a gingko leaf and has the inscription, "The imprint of a dying leaf is wondrous to behold." It was created by "Scopia," the partnership of sculptors Bill Severson and Saunders Schultz, while the garden was designed by the landscape architect Robert Goetz. The nearby overlook is dedicated to Chubb (1894–1977), a noted St. Louis attorney. The Chubb Pavilion, dedicated in 1981, was designed by landscape architect John Mareing and funded by friends of Walston Chubb.

The Golden Eagle River Museum occupied the Nims House from 1974 to 2004.

Bee Tree Park
Founded: 1968
Size: 199.34 acres

BUDER PARK

*B*uder Park, like Tilles and Fort Belle Fontaine, was once part of a projected St. Louis City park system within the county. Gustavus A. Buder Sr. and his wife, Lydia, gave seventy acres to the city in 1917 and another seventy acres the following year, specifying that it be called Buder Bathing Beach and Recreation Camp. In accepting the property, Mayor Henry Kiel wrote, "You have given us the property, and if it is not developed the fault will be mine." Plans for rental cottages and boathouses were announced but never implemented.

Gustavus Buder was a lawyer and publisher of the *St. Louis Times* and the German-language *Westliche Post* until the early 1930s and had many other business interests. The Buder family supported the city in many ways, including donating the Buder Playground at Hickory Street and California Avenue and added the Buder Recreation Center in 1930. The original Buder Branch Library opened in 1922. G. A. Buder Sr. died in 1954, and his will empowered his executors to recover the undeveloped park property from the city. They turned the land over to St. Louis County that same year.

The park's checkered history continued under the county. Over the years, the county has added more than sixty acres to the original Buder gift along the Meramec River and to the south. On the other hand, Interstate 44 divided the Buder tract into two parts. The southern portion, at the top of the Meramec Valley bluff, has become known as Upper Buder. It has picnic shelters and tennis courts. Lower Buder, because of its level, unobstructed ground, has attracted a variety of special events over the years, including steeplechase horse racing.

Lydia D. Buder Park
Founded: 1954
Size: 275.59 acres

CLIFF CAVE PARK

The cave for which this park is named has been a landmark in southern St. Louis County since the original settlement of the area, marked "Indian Cave" on nineteenth-century maps. The mouth of the cave opens directly out of the Mississippi River bluff about fifty feet high and was described in 1895 as being "like the door of some ancient cathedral." The land around it, however, remains nearly as it was in the 1840s. Speculators tried unsuccessfully to develop a subdivision called Cave Cliffs as early as 1857. A decade later, a dentist named Christopher W. Spalding organized the Cliff Cave Wine Company. He planted about twenty-five acres of vines and built a wall across the face of the cave to use it as a cool storage room. During this time, the Indian Cave became a popular destination for steamboat excursions. The *City of Alton* advertised in 1876, "Get on board and get out of the heat and dust of the city for one day at least." The Iron Mountain Railroad erected a station at the foot of the bluff.

The wine failed to make a profit, and the Pettus family acquired the property in 1877. They held it for nearly a century until the county purchased the land in 1972, using proceeds from the 1969 bond issue and federal matching funds.

At first the cave was open to spelunkers in good weather, but it was permanently closed after six people tragically drowned during one of the record rainfalls of 1993. The flood that year also damaged the low land between the railroad line and the river. It was subsequently elevated using fill provided by the nearby Bussen Quarry. Twin Hollow Associates donated 239 acres of riverside land south of the park to the county in 2003, and it was subsequently paved with three miles of trails.

Cliff Cave Park
Founded: 1972
Size: 525.86 acres

EBSWORTH PARK

Even in a park system that includes a transportation museum and a sculpture park, a park that includes a house designed by the great American architect Frank Lloyd Wright has to stand out as unusual. The park is named for Alec W. and Bernice W. Ebsworth, the parents of Barney A. Ebsworth, a St. Louis businessman and nationally known collector of American art. He gave more than half of the $1.7 million raised to purchase the property from Russell Kraus, the original owner. The Frank Lloyd Wright House in Ebsworth Park is one of only five buildings in Missouri designed by Wright (1867–1959). It is a "Usonian" house, the term Wright used for his smaller houses for people of modest means, but it is also one of his most complex designs, based on two overlapping parallelograms of 60 and 120 degrees. Wright designed all the furnishings, which still exist, including parallelogram beds and special studio equipment for Kraus, an artist and graphic designer. Russell and his wife, Ruth, started building in 1951, moved in at the beginning of 1956, and continued work on the interiors until 1962. Kraus designed the striking leaded glass doors, the latest example of art glass in any Wright house. The property was listed in the National Register of Historic Places in 1997 as the Russell and Ruth Goetz Kraus House.

Starting in 1995, Judy Bettendorf and others created a 501(c)3 organization, later headed by Joanne Kohn, which raised the funds for purchase, restoration, and management. The county took the title on January 18, 2001, and immediately leased the property back to the organization. Architect John Eifler, of Eifler & Associates of Chicago, supervised restoration of the house. The organization has continued to make improvements to the property, including paving the gravel entrance drive. Volunteer docents lead tours by appointment.

KENNEDY PARK

*O*riginally called South County Park, Kennedy was acquired and developed as one of three regional parks as a result of the $25 million bond issue passed by county voters in 1969. The others are Queeny Park to the west and Veterans Memorial Park to the north. The large recreation complex at the center of the park was designed by R. W. Booker & Associates.

The history of the land goes back to a 340-acre Spanish land grant, later confirmed by the U.S. government as Survey 993. Taken together, Kennedy Park and the adjacent Lower Meramec Park constitute the whole grant, perhaps the only such grant in St. Louis County to remain largely devoted to open space and in a single ownership. (A runner-up would be Survey 2507, now divided between Glen Echo Country Club and St. Vincent Park.)

The park was renamed in 1993 in honor of Wayne C. Kennedy. Originally a teacher and assistant principal with the Mehlville School District, Kennedy joined the county's Department of Parks and Recreation in 1961. Just a year later he was named director of the department, and he served until 1991. In his three decades with the county, he was able to increase park acreage from just over one thousand to nearly thirteen thousand.

In addition to the Kennedy Recreation Complex, the park includes the Quail Creek Golf Course, which opened in 1987. A new playground was completed in 2002, and lighted tennis courts and picnic sites are also available.

Wayne C. Kennedy Park
Founded: 1972
Size: 563.05 acres

LONE ELK PARK

*A*long with West Tyson Park, Lone Elk is a remnant of the 2,400-acre Tyson Valley Powder Plant used for the testing and storage of ammunition during World War II. After the war, the whole tract was transferred to St. Louis County for use as a county park, and in 1948 herds of elk and bison were established there. Just a short time later, however, the land was re-acquired by the federal government at the onset of the Korean Conflict, and for safety reasons the wildlife herds were destroyed in 1958. One lone bull elk somehow survived.

Many people assumed that the Tyson Valley site would eventually be returned to the county. But when the opportunity arose, Washington University made a counter proposal that carried the day. Through the efforts of Parks Director Wayne Kennedy, however, the county was able to reacquire 405 acres of the original tract in 1964 for $60,787. The name was changed in 1966 from Tyson Park to Lone Elk Park. Six additional elk were obtained from Yellowstone National Park that year through the efforts of the children of the Rockwood School District and West St. Louis County Lions Club. Six bison were acquired from the St. Louis Zoo in July 1973. Both the elk and the bison have gradually increased to substantial herds.

The World Bird Sanctuary, formerly the Raptor Rehabilitation and Propagation Project, occupied the Visitor Center at Lone Elk from 1986 to 2003.

Lone Elk Park
Founded: 1964
Size: 547.77 acres

ST. VINCENT PARK

The magnificent chateauesque building at the heart of St. Vincent Park is the former St. Vincent Hospital, built between 1892 and 1895 by the Daughters of Charity of St. Vincent de Paul to relocate their mental facility from the Soulard neighborhood. The architect was George R. Mann, who was working on the St. Louis City Hall at the same time, but the design was probably by Mann's employee Harvey Ellis, a celebrated talent of the time. The grounds around the hospital were used until the late 1940s by the nuns and patients to raise crops and graze cows and hogs for food.

The Daughters of Charity established their provincial house in 1914 on land north of the "Castle." The cemetery for the order opened in 1928, and Marillac College operated still further north from 1955 to 1974. The college and provincial house have been acquired by the University of Missouri–St. Louis. The hospital closed in June 1978, and the Daughters of Charity relocated their medical activities to the DePaul Community Health Center.

At that time, St. Louis County purchased the land around the hospital, supported by grants from the National Park Service. The Castle was not included in the park but was renovated as Castle Park Apartments. It was listed in the National Register of Historic Places in 1982.

The St. Vincent Community Center was opened in June 1989 as a result of the 1986 voter-approved bond issue monies. It has space for recreation programs, civic group meetings, and organized basketball and day camps at the facility. The water park was opened in 1994 with a water slide and eighty-foot flume ride. The playground was redeveloped in 2001. Acquisition of a small parcel on the east side of Salerno Drive in 2003 has permitted creation of a loop trail around the Castle.

SIOUX PASSAGE PARK

*T*he land that has become Sioux Passage Park was purchased in 1965 with money from a bond issue, but its history goes back to the Late Woodland and Mississippian periods. Sioux Passage Park Archaeological Site was listed in the National Register of Historic Places in 1974.

The park is one of few places in the county with a wide public access to the Missouri River. Early explorers passed here, and the journal of Zebulon Pike refers to camping in this vicinity. Steamboats began to ply the river in the 1820s, and one of them, the *Car of Commerce*, foundered and sank near here in 1832, giving its name to the passage of the river called the Car of Commerce Chute.

Beyond the chute is Pelican Island, a tract of nearly two thousand acres given to St. Louis County by Joseph Desloge and deeded by the county to the Missouri Department of Conservation in 1991 but never officially opened to the public.

John D. Briscoe Park is a tract of thirty-three acres adjacent to the entrance to Sioux Passage Park on Old Jamestown Road and almost indistinguishable from it. John Briscoe bequeathed the property to the county as an act of civic generosity in 2002. The land had been farmed by Mrs. Briscoe's grandfather and other members of the family for a century, but it is now being returned to a natural condition.

Sioux Passage Park
Founded: 1965
Size: 211.6 acres

John D. Briscoe Park
Founded: 2002
Size: 37.68 acres

SUSON PARK

The original Suson tract was purchased by the county from Sidney Salomon Jr. in 1962. He was a well-known figure in St. Louis at the time as owner of the old Sportsman's Park. His fame increased in 1966 when he acquired the Arena and became the first owner of the St. Louis Blues hockey team. The name of this park originated with Salomon as a combination of his children's names, Susan and Sonny.

Suson Park was intended to be a farm park from the outset, and because several of the buildings and the five lakes were already in existence when the land was purchased, both the animal farm and the lake fishing attractions were available when the park opened in 1964. The large new barn was constructed with funds from the 1969 bond issue. County Parks dredged the largest lake in 1978, creating a new depth of ten feet from the original one to three feet. The Missouri Department of Conservation stocks this lake. O'Fallon Brothers Construction Company deeded ten more acres to the park in 1980.

Suson Park draws its land from several different nineteenth-century farms, but the main part of the park belonged to Frederick Hagemann, who sold it to Julius Riepe in about 1872. Riepe built the old brick house at the center of the park, now painted white with many later additions.

Most types of animals typical to Missouri farms can be seen at Suson, including draft horses and dairy cattle.

Suson Park
Founded: 1962
Size: 97.44 acres

VETERANS MEMORIAL

*L*ike Queeny and Wayne C. Kennedy parks, Veterans Memorial Park resulted from the passage by the voters of a $25 million bond issue in 1969. The county bought 227.40 acres of the present park the next year. The recreation complex was constructed in 1976, designed by the architectural firm, Hastings & Chivetta. The building was substantially renovated from 2009 to 2011, when the indoor skating rink was replaced by a multi-purpose gymnasium.

The present park constitutes almost 40 percent of a historic mile-square (640-acre) tract known as Survey 2495, claimed by William Robertson, a farmer from New Madrid County, as compensation for damages sustained in the great New Madrid earthquakes of 1811 and 1812. Redman Road, named for local farmer C. B. Redman, follows the southern boundary of the survey, and Parker Road follows the northern boundary.

The idea of a golf course at Veterans Park was broached as early as 1973, and construction specifications were drawn up in 1977 by David Gill, a golf course architect. The present Eagle Springs Golf Course was not authorized by the County Council until 1986, however.

COUNTY PARKS

*I*n addition to the twenty-two parks already described, St. Louis County's park system includes the following twenty-three parks in active use. At least that many more sites are undeveloped, awaiting future planning, or leased to other entities, public and private. The geographical and functional range of these parks reflects the dual nature of the county system, serving both as a regional park system and, in lieu of a municipal park system, for the unincorporated county, providing smaller neighborhood parks and playgrounds, particularly in the north and south regions. As parts of the county have incorporated, at least eighteen additional parks have been transferred by the county to other agencies.

NORTH

Bella Fontaine, *19565 Bellefontaine Rd., Bellefontaine Neighbors*	209.93 acres
Bon Oak, *Champlin and Doane Drs.*	15.31 acres
Castle Point, *2465 Baroness Dr.*	10.78 acres
Norman B. Champ, *3991 Grand National Dr.*	101.38 acres
Endicott, *2950 Endicott Ave., St. John*	24.04 acres
Martin Luther King, Jr. Memorial, *1491 Dielman Rd.*	4.01 acres
Kinloch, *Smith and Bangert, Kinloch*	9.23 acres
Larimore, *11726 Larimore Rd.*	24.54 acres
McDonnell, *2961 Adie Rd., St. Ann*	133.21 acres

WEST

John Allen Love, *2239 Mason Lane, nr. Manchester*	89.03 acres
Memorial, *County Gov't Center, 41 South Central, Clayton*	2.68 acres
Ohlendorf West, *1150 Hanna Rd., nr. Valley Park*	46.07 acres
West Tyson, *131 North Outer Rd., nr. Eureka*	672.57 acres

SOUTH

Affton-White Rodgers Community Center, *9801 Mackenzie Rd.*	7.98 acres
Black Forest, *9822 Perrin Ave.*	4.25 acres
George H. Bohrer, *5700 South Lindbergh*	16.48 acres
Clydesdale, *9517 Green Park Rd., Green Park*	117.96 acres
Lemay, *234 Military Rd.*	18.46 acres
Mathilda-Welmering, *8315 Mathilda Ave.*	6.19 acres
Ohlendorf, *4400 Spring Ave., nr. Union Rd.*	10.03 acres
Simpson, *1220 Marshall Rd., Valley Park*	175 acres
Unger, *410 Club Rd., on Meramec River nr. Fenton*	94.85 acres
George Winter, *401 Allen Rd., Fenton*	159.73 acres

Welcome to the Native Grassland and Wildflowers of Bon Oak Park

St. Louis County Parks has planted more than 20 species of wildflowers and grasses in 2 acres to provide for wildlife, add the color of native flowers, and reduce the overall mowing of the park.

MUNICIPAL PARKS

Almost forty of St. Louis County's ninety-one cities and villages maintain at least one park or playground. Some of these municipal parks predate the county's park system. In University City, for example, voters established a park board in 1922 and the following year approved a bond issue that paid for five parks, including the ninety-three-acre Heman Park. Since then, University City has established a park to honor each of its outgoing mayors. The city of Clayton acquired fifty-one acres in 1935 and developed it with WPA grants, naming it Shaw Park for its mayor at the time.

The majority of municipal parks are neighborhood playgrounds. Ten of these were originally created by County Parks and subsequently transferred to a locality, such as Tanglewood Park in Bellefontaine Neighbors and Vinita County Park, the namesake for Vinita Park neighborhood. Only a few municipal parks approach a hundred acres. Bluebird Park in Ellisville has 167.36 acres, but that includes the 67.42-acre Klamberg Woods, which is actually owned by the Conservation Department. Kirkwood Park extends to 92 acres and Florissant's Sunset Park to 90 acres.

Most municipal parks have been paid for by tax revenues, and St. Louis County voters have a proud record of supporting parks at the polls. One notable example is Wild Acres Park in Overland, 31.25 acres at Midland and Ashby, rescued from development by the citizens in 1995. Several of the larger cities have invested substantially in recreation complexes, which are seen as enhancing the desirability of the community and giving it a special identity. Another source of community identity has been the preservation of historic houses in parks. The Payne-Gentry House in Bridgeton, Hanley House in Clayton, Sappington House in Crestwood, and Hawken House in Webster Groves are all located in city parks. Black Jack and Crestwood are notable among cities that also maintain historic cemeteries, both for their scenic beauty and their historic significance.

MUNICIPALITIES MAINTAINING PARKS

Ballwin
Bellefontaine Neighbors
Bel Ridge
Berkeley
Black Jack
Breckenridge Hills
Brentwood
Bridgeton
Chesterfield
Clayton
Country Club Hills
Crestwood
Creve Coeur
Dellwood
Des Peres
Edmundson
Ellisville
Eureka
Fenton
Ferguson

Florissant
Hazelwood
Jennings
Kirkwood
Manchester
Maplewood
Maryland Heights
Normandy
Northwoods
Olivette
Overland
Riverview
St. Ann
St. George
Shrewsbury
Sunset Hills
University City
Vinita Park
Webster Groves

STATE PARKS

Missouri's state parks are part of the Department of Natural Resources, or DNR, which also directs historic preservation and environmental protection. In St. Louis County, the department has three parks: Dr. Edmund A. Babler Memorial State Park is a tract of over 2,100 acres of forest in Wildwood. Jacob and Henry Babler presented it to the state in 1934 in memory of their brother. The park's pavilions and other facilities were built by the Civilian Conservation Corps, a New Deal program, and are listed in the National Register of Historic Places.

The Castlewood area west of Valley Park along the Meramec River has attracted St. Louisans since the Missouri Pacific Railroad first offered easy access in 1853. Castlewood State Park was created in 1974 to protect this resort-like area. Its 1,818 acres along both sides of the Meramec River include palisade bluffs and river floodplain. The Chubb Trail follows the south bank of the river, while the Al Foster Trail follows the north. The World Bird Sanctuary is at the south end of the site. Castlewood is a central element of the Meramec Greenway, which has created a greenbelt along the river, including several county and municipal parks and Washington University's Tyson Research Center.

Route 66 State Park is also part of the Meramec Greenway a few miles upstream of Castlewood near Eureka. The *St. Louis Times* newspaper promoted residential development there, originally for weekend "clubhouses" or private cottages. Times Beach soon became a year-round town of modest residences and unpaved streets. Dioxin contamination from the oil used to control dust on the streets forced the removal of the entire town in the 1990s. Route 66 State Park was created on the site of the cleanup in 1997. Its 418 acres commemorate the "Mother Road," one of America's most celebrated highways, which has traversed the area since 1931. The visitors center in the old roadhouse includes historical exhibits and a shop with Route 66 memorabilia. The historic bridge spanning the Meramec has been closed, but hopes for its restoration persist.

MISSOURI DEPARTMENT OF CONSERVATION

*L*ike many other states, Missouri has two departments concerned with open space. State parks are in the Department of Natural Resources while state conservation areas are in the Department of Conservation. Conservation owns or leases more than twelve thousand acres in St. Louis County, almost as much as County Parks. Conservation also maintain the lakes in several municipal parks in Ballwin, Fenton, Ferguson, Kirkwood, and in ten county parks.

A. P. Greensfelder, who was the catalyst for so many open-space initiatives in this area, introduced the Department of Conservation to the county in 1938, when he and a group of friends presented the 1,880-acre Rockwoods Reservation, followed in 1943 by a personal gift of another 1,388 acres for the Rockwoods Range. Holdings increased in 1990 with Pelican Island, 2,260 acres, transferred from the county (originally a gift of Joseph Desloge), 812 acres of the old St. Stanislaus Seminary property leased from the county, and the nearly 1,000-acre Forest 44 tract acquired after a public campaign. The city of St. Louis transferred its 4,300-acre Columbia Bottom property in 1997, part of the larger project to protect the confluence of the Missouri and Mississippi rivers.

The Powder Valley Conservation Nature Center in Kirkwood, a popular resource for education, celebrated its twentieth anniversary in 2011. Conservation also maintains nearly a dozen other areas, some as small as ten acres. Elizabeth Gempp, Joan Goodson, Minna Waldmann, and Ray and Claire Moore are among the civic-minded property owners who have contributed their land for public benefit.

BIBLIOGRAPHY

Annual Reports of the St. Louis Parks Department. Acreage, cost of purchase and improvements, construction and maintenance projects, and usage figures were found in these reports, 1893–1948.

Atlas of the City of St. Louis, Missouri. Philadelphia: G.M. Hopkins, C.E., 1883.

Banner, Stuart. *Legal Systems in Conflict, Property and Sovereignty in Missouri, 1750-1860.* Norman: University of Oklahoma Press, 1998.

Carondelet Park tree survey completed in April 2007 by Skip Kincaid & Associates (SKA).

The Civic League of Saint Louis. *A Plan for Saint Louis, Reports of the Several Committees Appointed by the Executive Board of the Civic League to Draft a City Plan,* 1907.

Cotton, Jr., W. Philip. *Clifton Heights, Preliminary Neighborhood Historical Research Report.* St. Louis: Heritage/St. Louis, 1971.

Clipping files on the St. Louis Parks, History Department, St. Louis Public Library, Main Branch.

Commonfields Map of St. Louis, redrawn by the National Park Service from the Huttawa Atlas, a compilation of 1848.

Dacus, J.A., and James W. Buel. *A Tour of St. Louis or, the Inside Life of a Great City.* St. Louis: Western Publishing Company, Jones & Griffin, 1878.

Darby, John F. *Personal Recollections of John F. Darby, Mayor of St. Louis, 1835, Sketches of Prominent People and of Events Relating to the History of St. Louis During the First Half of the Nineteenth Century.* St. Louis: G.I. Jones and Company, 1880.

Dates, Donald. Scrapbooks of Carondelet History, compiled 1945-1947.

"Don't Despoil Lafayette Park," *St. Louis Star,* August 5, 1927, editorial, Clipping file of St. Louis Public Library.

Dry, Camille N., and Rich. J. Compton. *Pictorial St. Louis, Metropolis of the Mississippi Valley, A Topographical Survey,* 1875.

Hill, Sarah Full. *Mrs. Hill's Journal-Civil War Reminiscences,* edited by Mark M. Krug. Chicago: The Lakeside Press, 1980.

Mayor's Messages. Biannual reports containing references to the parks, and sometimes reports on individual parks, prior to the 1876 separation of the City and County.

Orear, G.W. *Commercial and Architectural St. Louis.* St. Louis: Jones & Orear Publishers, 1888.

Pape, Fred W., Commissioner of Parks and Recreation of the City of St. Louis. "Francis Park Destined to be One of the Beauty Spots of St. Louis," *City Beautiful*, April 1930.

Park report dated November 1874 included in Mayor's Message of January 1875.

The Past in Our Presence: Historic Buildings in St. Louis County. St. Louis County, Missouri, 1996.

Pitzman, Julius. *Pitzman's New Atlas of the City and County of Saint Louis Missouri.* Philadelphia: A.B. Holcombe & Co., 1878.

Reavis, L.U. *Saint Louis: The Future Great City of the World.* St. Louis: Gray, Baker & Co., 1875.

St. Louis Area Cemeteries, compiled by the Microfilm Department and the History and Genealogy Departments of St. Louis Public Library, April 2005.

Saint Louis Illustrated: Her Public Buildings, Churches, Press, Parks, Gardens, People, Schools, Railroads, Commerce, Manufactories, Etc. St. Louis: Will Conklin, 1876.

Scharf, J. Thomas. *History of St. Louis City and County, from the Earliest Periods to the Present Day.* Philadelphia: Louis H. Everts & Co., 1883.

Souvenir of Carondelet, a promotional booklet published in the early 1890s.

Wells, Rolla. *Episodes of My Life.* St. Louis, 1933.

"World's Largest Open Air Swimming Pool Draws Half Million," *Forward St. Louis*, May 4, 1914.

INDEX OF FEATURED PARKS

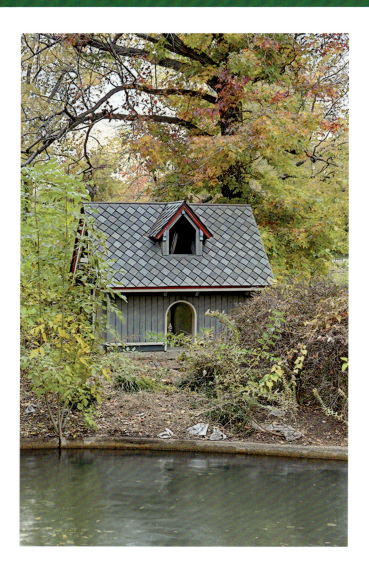

ABOUT THE AUTHORS AND PHOTOGRAPHERS

NiNi Harris's earliest memory is of an early autumn evening, picking up acorns as she and her father walked along Bellerive Boulevard to Bellerive Park. Her great-great-grandfather's first job when he arrived in St. Louis in 1864 was planting trees in a St. Louis park. This is her tenth book on St. Louis history and architecture.

Esley Hamilton has been working for the St. Louis County Department of Parks and Recreation as historian and preservationist since 1977. Among preservationists in the St. Louis region, Hamilton's is a household name. He teaches the history of landscape architecture at Washington University and serves on the board of the National Association for Olmsted Parks.

Mark Abeln is a native of St. Louis and attended college at Caltech, in Pasadena, California. Mark started taking photography seriously after he took disappointing photos of an important subject. He spent the next years learning the art of photography, and his photos can now be found in numerous publications as well as on his website "Rome of the West."

Steve Tiemann graduated from McCluer High School and went on to obtain his forestry degree from the University of Missouri at Columbia. Steve has enjoyed his career with the St. Louis County Park Rangers for nearly thirty years and always has a camera at hand to capture those magic moments in the beautiful outdoors.